# BOAR HO

Matthew Rich

*All coin die drawings by the author.*
*Edited by Elizabeth Cottam and Chris Rudd.*

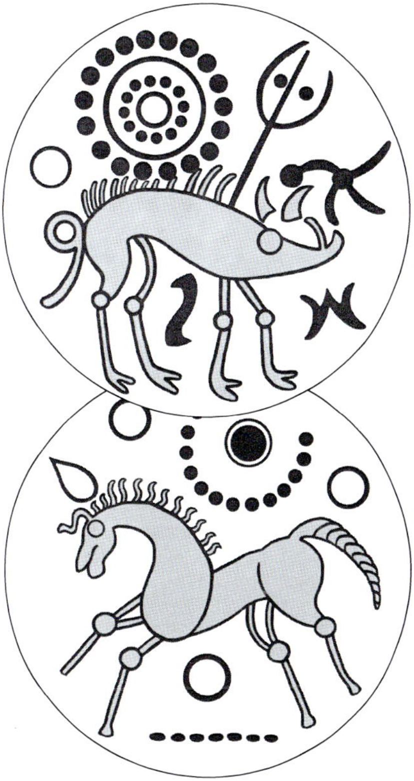

Chris Rudd
PO Box 222 Aylsham Norfolk NR11 6TY

*Publisher* CHRIS RUDD AYLSHAM 2014



*Designer* Brendan Rallison, email: studio@brendanrallison.co.uk

*Printer* Page Bros (Norwich) Ltd, Mile Cross Lane,
Norwich, Norfolk NR6 6SA
Tel: 01630 778800 Web: www.pagebros.co.uk

*Distributor* This book can be ordered directly from:
Chris Rudd , PO Box 222, Aylsham, Norfolk NR11 6TY.
Tel: 01263 735 007. Fax: 01263 731 777.
Email: liz@celticcoins.com

A catalogue record for *Boar Horse* is available from the British Library.

*ISBN* 978-0-9566889-2-7

Matthew Rich was born in South Africa 1938 and emigrated to Australia 1975 where he was Chief Financial Officer of a publishing company in Sydney. His interest in numismatics was sparked by seeing Roman coins for sale while on a business visit to London in 1970. Assuming that the coins were replicas he was astonished to find that there were real. Thus began a lifelong interest in coins. Firstly Roman coins, then Crusader coins and finally Ancient British coins. His interest in the Ancient British series was there from the start, but examples were almost completely unavailable in the 70's and only to be viewed with longing in Seaby's coin guide at astronomical prices. But the advent of the metal detector, and Chris Rudd's coin lists in the early 1990's, soon changed all that and Ancient British coins were suddenly plentiful and affordable, supported by the timely publication of Robert Van Ardell's *Celtic Coinage of Britain* in 1989. On retirement Matthew Rich continued collecting and decided, with the encouragement of Dr Philip de Jersey, to study the silver coinage of the Corieltavi in the hope that he could in some small measure give back something to the hobby that gave him so much pleasure. *Boar Horse* is his gift to fellow students.

# Contents




## Thank you!

We thank Martin Bridgewater for photos of Corieltavian silver units and half units from his incomparable collection of Ancient British coins: front cover and figs. **6, 7, 8, 9, 10, 15, 16, 17, 18, 23, 24, 25, 27, 29**. For their superb pictures we also thank these people: **1** lithograph of Witham Shield from *Horae Ferales* by John Kemble, enhanced by BR; drawing of Rothwell Boar by Jane Bottomley. **4** lithograph of coin from *L'Art Gaulois* by Eugène Hucher; photo of Deskford carnyx reconstruction, National Museums of Scotland. **5** drawing of Farnsfield mount by Jane Bottomley. **14** photo of Rothwell Boar courtesy of Antony Lee, The Collection, Lincoln Museum. **21** drawing of reconstructed pellet mould tray by Margaret Jones in *Old Sleaford Revealed* by Sheila M.Elsdon; photos of mould fragments by Wardell Armstrong Archaeology in *Current Archaeology* 292, July 2014. **26** photo of Heckington Stag by BS. **30** coin drawing by Léon Dardel in *Atlas de monnaies gauloises* by Henri de la Tour, 1892. **31** coin drawing by Sue White. All other illustrations, maps, diagrams and tables in *Boar Horse* were produced by the author and/or publisher. We apologise for any omissions of acknowledgement.

# Foreword

The wild boar must have been important to the Iron Age peoples of the East Midlands. It can be seen not only on their earliest silver coins, but also on a shield, on a war trumpet and as a small figurine. Symbolising bravery in battle, the boar was probably a tribal emblem of the Corieltavi – an apt mascot for a tribe whose name means 'army of the broad land' or 'army (of the goddess) Litavis'. The horse too was important to the Corieltavi for it occurs on virtually all their coins – gold as well as silver – often in a highly stylised form.

In *Boar Horse* numismatist Matthew Rich shows how these two iconic animals were displayed on the first silver coins of the Corieltavi. His enlarged drawings, detailed descriptions and die analysis of 123 coin types and sub types clearly demonstrate how this series developed. *Boar Horse* makes identification easy. We think it will appeal not only to scholars, collectors and metdets, but also to anyone interested in the prehistory and pre-Roman art of the East Midlands.

Elizabeth Cottam
Chris Rudd
Aylsham, Lughnasad 2014

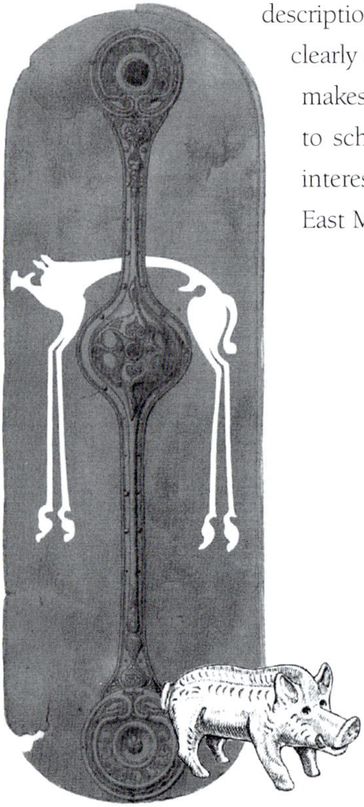

1. *The Witham Shield bronze-facing (100cm high) emblazoned with emblematic Corieltavian boar, and the Rothwell Boar bronze figurine (5.5cm long), both from Lincs. Tribal symbols weren't confined to tribal coins.*

# Introduction

## The Corieltavi

The Corieltavi were an Iron Age tribe, or more probably a loose federation of different tribes, living mainly within the area of modern Lincolnshire (extending partially into Nottinghamshire, Leicestershire, Northamptonshire and Cambridgeshire) with the natural boundaries of the River Trent in the west and the River Nene in the south.

The Romans later developed two of their major sites, Lincoln (*Lindum*) and Leicester (*Ratae Coritanorum*) but there were numerous Iron Age settlements throughout the area including Dragonby, Kirmington, South Ferriby, Ludford and Caistor in the north and Partney and Ulceby Cross in the south.

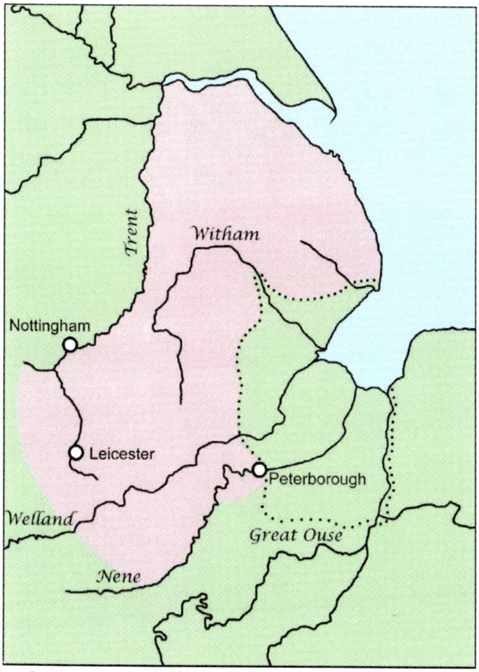


2. *Territory occupied by the Corieltavi according to the coin evidence ( ········ Iron Age shoreline)*

The Corieltavi struck an extensive coinage in gold and silver, but not in bronze, from about 60 BC until the Roman conquest in 43 AD. The earliest gold coins were based on Gallo-Belgic Type C staters (ABC 13) and developed a vigorous and individual style quite different from the coinage struck elsewhere by other Iron Age tribes.

The silver coinage is no less distinctive and the uninscribed boar/horse series is a long and complex one generally regarded as covering the period from about 60 BC until the introduction of inscribed coins in about 10 AD[1] although production may have continued as late as AD 30 not long before the Roman invasion[2].

The earliest coins of this type were probably derived from an unlikely prototype, a Roman Republican issue C.Hosidius C.f. Geta[3] struck in 68 BC, which depicts the Calydonian boar with a spear impaled in its back. While the inspiration may have been Roman, the series rapidly developed its own distinctive local style.

*Crawford 407/1*

A notable stylistic characteristic is the use of the bifurcated leg: i.e. the horse (almost always) and boar (commonly) is shown with the upper part of the forelegs in an outline Y shape. This feature, apart from limited use by the neighbouring Iceni, is unique to this tribe and is used, with various modifications, throughout the series.

The sequencing of the series can be demonstrated by the stylistic evolution of the boar on the obverse and the horse on the reverse.

**3.** *Silver denarius of C.Hosidius C.f. Geta, 68 BC, Sear RCV 346. Diana, seen here with bow and quiver at her shoulder, sent the Calydonian boar to ravage the lands of Aetolia in revenge for the neglect shown to her by King Oeneus. The speared boar is being attacked by a hunting dog.*

## The Boar

The **Early Period** of the series starts with a pierced boar with solid front and rear legs **(A)**, progressing to a pierced boar with a bifurcated left rear leg **(B)** followed by an unpierced boar with both forelegs bifurcated in a W shape **(C)**. In the next **Intermediate Period** the boar has bifurcated left legs shown alternately **(D)** or centrally **(E)**. The subsequent **Middle Period** starts with a boar with bifurcated forelegs and solid rear legs **(F)** before the forelegs of the boar are finally combined into a single Y shape **(G)**. In the **Late Period** the obverse dies become completely obliterated.

**A**
*Early period*

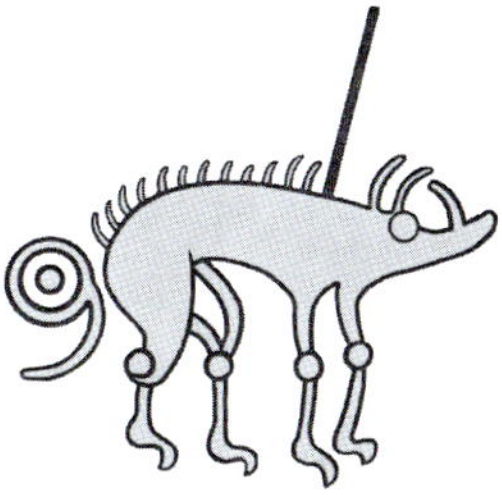

**B**
*Early period*

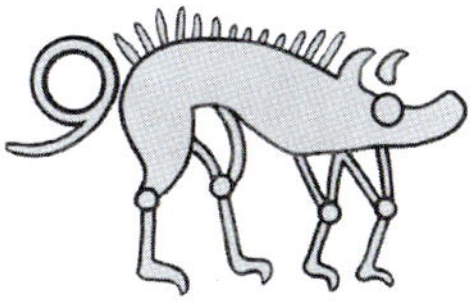

**C**
*Early period*

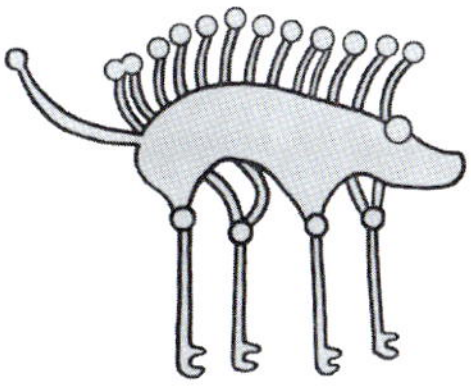

**D**
*Intermediate period*

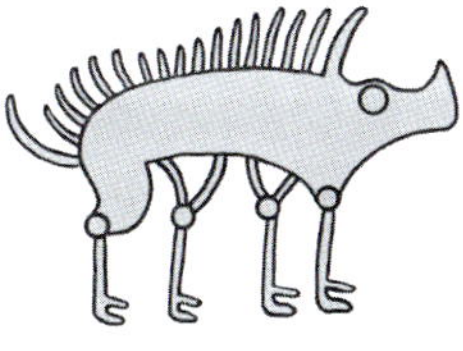

**E**
*Intermediate period*

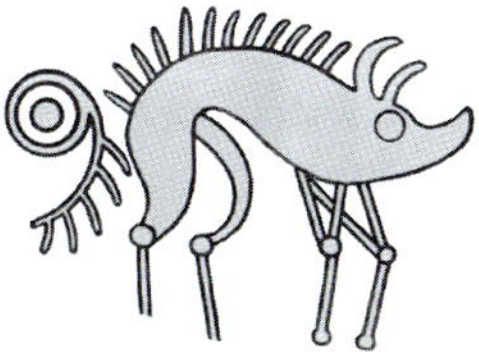

**F**
*Middle period*

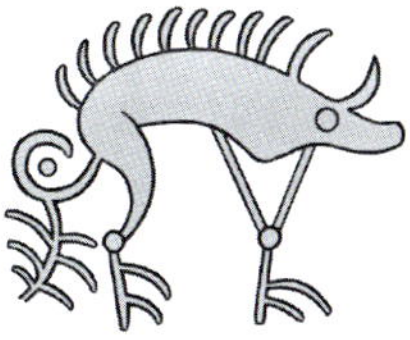

**G**
*Middle period*

With one exception **(Type 23)** the boar always faces right. There is a rare variation with the boar replaced by a wolf **(Type 8)**.

4. *In Britain and Gaul the boar was often linked to warfare. Silver coin of Aedui, c.70-50 BC, LT 5044, with boar-standard and boar-mouthed war-trumpet similar to one found in river Witham, Lincs., and another from Deskford, Banff. (reconstruction illustrated).*

# The Horse

The horse, with one exception **(Type 6)**, always has bifurcated forelegs and often one bifurcated rear leg, and faces either left or right. The main aids to identification are to be found in the shape of the tail and, later in the series, in the shape of the head.

The **Early Period** starts with a handsome horse in classical style with a braided tail **(A)** followed by a horse with a leaf shaped tail **(B)**. The horse throughout the **Intermediate Period** has a short or long fern shaped tail **(C)**. In the **Middle Period** the horse always has a simple tail **(D)** sometimes stranded at the end **(F)** and the horse may be in shown in a kneeling position **(E)**. During the **Late Period** the uniface coins portray the horse in three styles: with a natural head **(G)** followed by a stork head **(H)** and a triangular head **(I)**. In these latter stages the forelegs often assume exaggerated proportions.

**A**
*Early period*
*Braided tail*

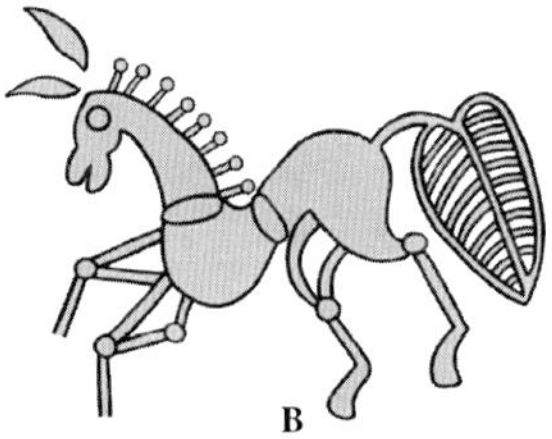

**B**
*Early period*
*Leaf tail*

**C**
*Intermediate period*
*Fern tail*

**D**
*Middle period*
*Simple tail*

**E**
*Middle period*
*Kneeling horse*

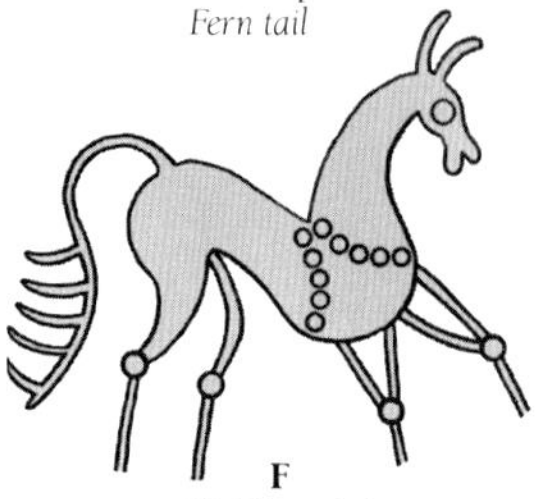

**F**
*Middle period*
*Stranded tail*

**G**
*Late period*
*natural head*

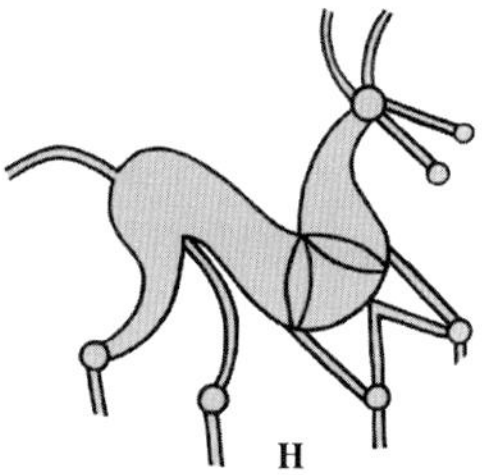

**H**
*Late period*
*stork head*

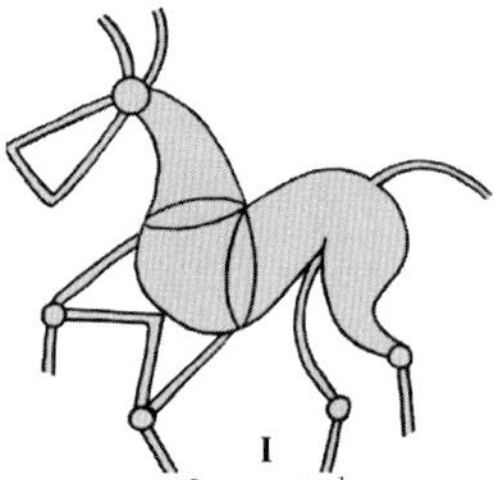

**I**
*Late period*
*triangular head*

## Half Units

Half units were introduced in the **Middle Period** during the issue of units **Type 24** and consequently exhibit only the later features of the boar and horse.

The boar may face right or left and all non-obliterated examples have the combined Y shape forelegs of type F **(HA)**. The horse also faces right or left with a natural head and simple tail **(HB)**.

Like the corresponding units, the horse on the **Late Period** uniface coins is portrayed in three distinct styles: with a natural head **(HC)**, a stork head **(HD)** or a triangular head. **(HE)**.

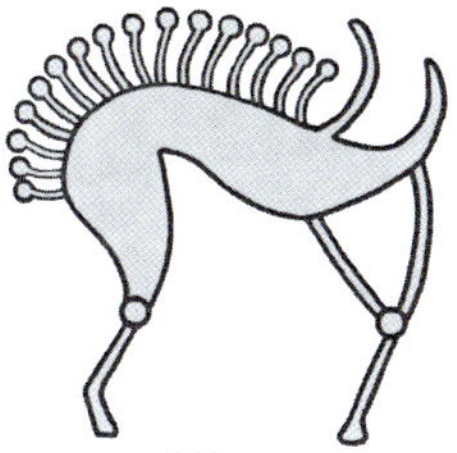

**HA**
*Middle period*

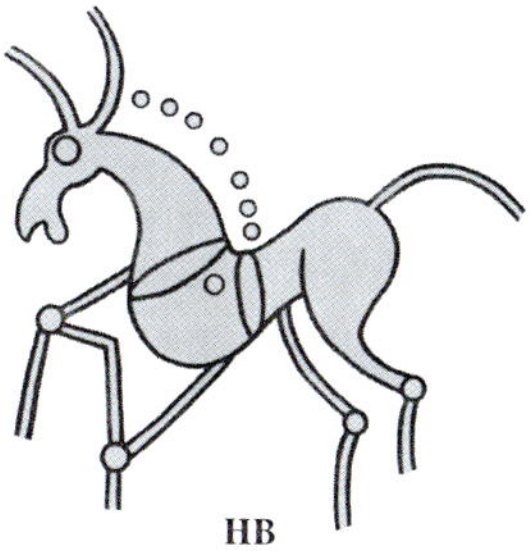

**HB**
*Middle period*

**HC**
*Late period*
*natural head*

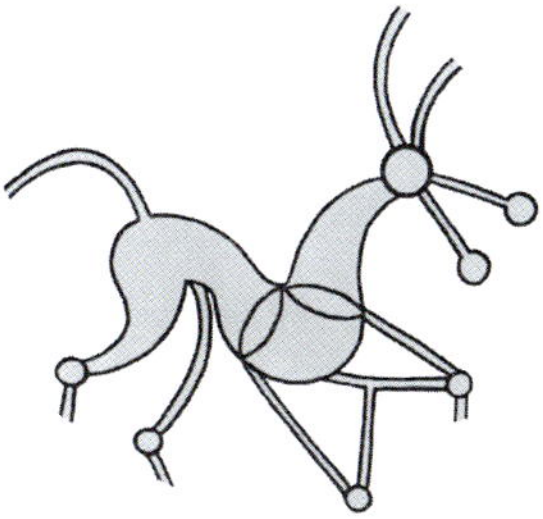

**HC**
*Late period*
*stork head*

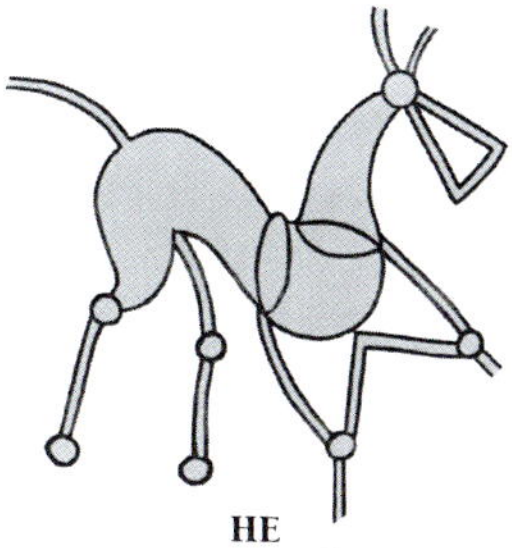

**HE**
*Late period*
*triangular head*

5. *Horses were highly prized in the Iron Age and served as male status symbols, like cars do today (the word 'car' comes from Celtic* carros *'chariot'). Rich men decorated their horses with costly enamelled horse 'brasses', like this bronze trefoil mount from Farnsfield, Lincs.*

**6.** *What is the meaning of the symbols on Iron Age coins? We can but guess. For example, is the boar pierced by a spear or by an arrow? Or is it a sun-sceptre, as suggested by John Hooker? Is the complex rosette above the boar a sun-sign? Is that a stylised serpent below the boar? What does the four-armed spiral signify? And what is that bat-like W-shape before the boar? It seems unlikely that such icons were randomly selected as mere ornaments. For those in the know – rulers, die cutters, priests? – each symbol may have had several layers of meaning, both sacred and secular. Rich Type 1a, Serpent Proto Boar.*

# Catalogue of unit types

## Type 1 Serpent Proto Boar

**Pierced boar right with solid legs, serpent below.**

**Horse left with braided tail.**

---

1a

VA 855-3   BMC 3194-3195

- 3 rings around horse
- 'teardrop' above horse's head

*24 examples in the CCI*
*6 obverse dies, 7 reverse dies*
*Illustrated: dies 6/5*

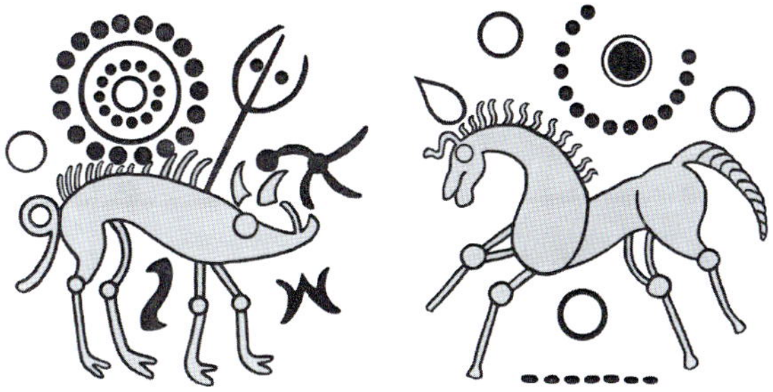

---

1b

BMC 3196

- 3 ringed pellets around horse

*15 examples in the CCI*
*2 obverse dies (1 from type 1a)*
*4 reverse dies*
*Illustrated: dies 6/8*

---

## Type 2 S-Type Proto Boar

**Pierced boar right with one bifurcated fore and rear leg, S below.**

**Horse left with braided tail.**

---

2

ABC 1779   BMC 3201

- S has pellet terminals
- ringed pellet below horse

*23 examples in the CCI*
*3 obverse dies, 7 reverse dies*
*Illustrated: dies 8/17*

# Type 3 Wishbone Proto Boar

**Pierced boar right with solid forelegs & one bifurcated rear leg, nothing below.**

**Horse left with braided tail.**

---

3a

- 'wishbone' above boar's head
- 3 ringed pellets around horse

*5 examples in the CCI*
*1 obverse die, 2 reverse dies*
*Illustrated: dies 11/19*

---

3b

VA 855-8

- elongated 'wishbone' above boar's head
- ringed pellets below horse's head & below

*5 examples in the CCI*
*1 obverse die, 2 reverse dies*
*Illustrated: dies 12/21*

---

3c

- elongated 'wishbone' above boar's head
- ringed pellet below horse

*1 example in the CCI*
*obverse die from Type 3b*
*Illustrated: dies 12/23*

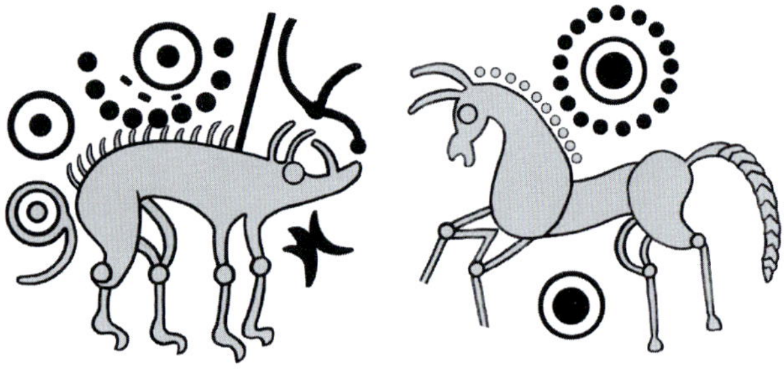

## **Type 4** X-Type Proto Boar

**Unpierced boar right with W shaped forelegs, X above head, nothing below.**

**Horse left with braided tail.**

---

4a

VA 855-7 BMC 3202

- right upper foreleg of boar has distinct 'elbow'
- ringed pellet below horse

*13 examples in the CCI*
*1 obverse die, 2 reverse dies*
*Illustrated: dies 13/24*

---

4b

- right upper foreleg of boar has distinct 'elbow'
- ringed pellets below horse's head & below

*4 examples in the CCI*
*2 obverse dies (1 from Type 4a)*
*3 reverse dies (2 from Type 3b) Illustrated: dies 13/22*

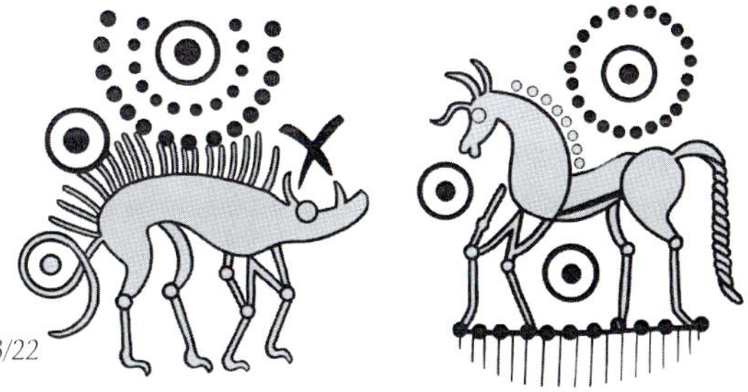

---

## **Type 5** S-Triad Proto Boar

**Unpierced boar right with W shaped forelegs, S triad above tail.**

**Horse left with braided tail.**

---

5a

- nothing below boar
- upper right foreleg is curved
- ringed pellets above horse's head & below

*13 examples in the CCI*
*2 obverse dies, 4 reverse dies*
*Illustrated: dies 15/28*

### 5b

- S below boar
- upper right foreleg is straight
- 3 ringed pellets around horse

*4 examples in the CCI*
*1 obverse die, 1 reverse die*
*Illustrated: dies 17/31*

---

### 5c

**ABC 1782**

- as 5b but ringed pellets above & below horse

*1 example in the CCI*
*obverse die from Type 5b*
*Illustrated: dies 17/29*

---

### 5d

- as 5b but ringed pellets below horse's head & below

*6 examples in the CCI*
*2 obverse dies*
*1 reverse die from Type 3b*
*Illustrated: dies 19/22*

---

### 5e

- as 5b but 1 ringed pellet below horse

*2 examples in the CCI*
*1 obverse die from Type 5d*
*1 reverse die from Type 3c*
*Illustrated: dies 19/23*

5f

- as 5e but ringed double-pellet within pellet ring above horse

*2 examples in the CCI*
*1 obverse die from Type 5d*
*1 reverse die*
*Illustrated: dies 19/32*

---

## Type 6 Sun & Moon Proto Boar

**Pierced boar right with solid legs.**

**Horse left with long thin tail.**

---

6a

BMC 3197

- 'sun & moon' above boar's rump
- S below boar
- 'sun & moon' below horse

*7 examples in the CCI*
*1 obverse die, 5 reverse dies*
*Illustrated: dies 20/33*

---

6b

- boar is a degraded version of 1a
- 'sun & moon' below horse

*1 example in the CCI*
*Illustrated: dies 21/38*

6c

- boar is a degraded version of 1a
- ring in pellet circle below horse

*1 example in the CCI*
*obverse die from Type 6b*
*Illustrated: dies 21/39*

---

## Type 7 Crown Proto Boar

**Boar right with W shaped forelegs, double arch above.**

**Horse left with pronounced leaf tail.**

---

7a

ABC 1785 VA 864-1 BMC 3213

- nothing below horse

*15 examples in the CCI*
*4 obverse dies, 6 reverse dies.*
*Illustrated: dies 25/44*

---

7b

- ringed pellet below horse

*8 examples in the CCI*
*3 obverse dies (1 from Type 1a)*
*3 reverse dies*
*Illustrated: dies 25/46*

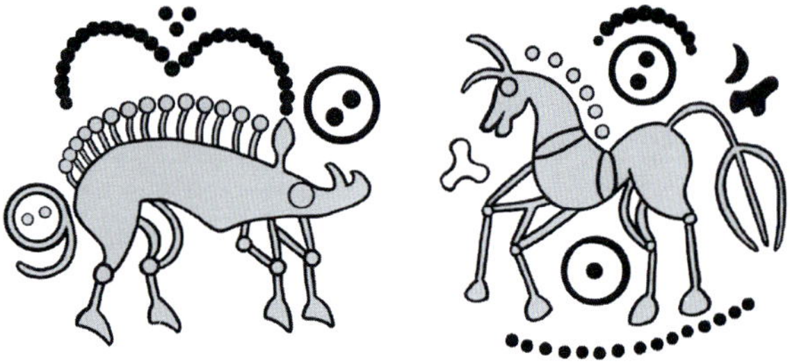

---

7c

- ringed double-pellet below horse

*5 examples in the CCI*
*1 obverse die from Type 7a*
*2 reverse dies*
*Illustrated: dies 25/49*

## Type 8 Lincolnshire Wolf

**Wolf right.**

**Horse left with leaf tail.**

8

ABC 1788 BMC 3205-3206

- 3 large ringed pellets above wolf
- ringed pellet triad above horse

*7 examples in the CCI*
*1 obverse die, 2 reverse dies.*
*Illustrated: dies 28/52*

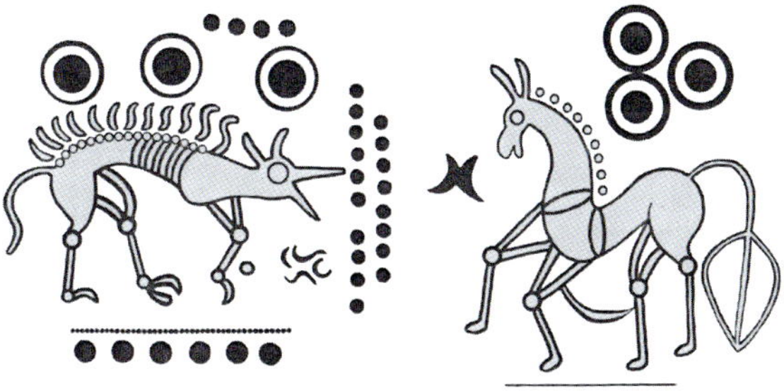

## Type 9 Three-Pellet Proto Boar

**Boar right with solid right legs and bifurcated left legs (with later variations).**

**Horse left with long fern tail.**

9a

VA 855-5

- ringed pellet-triangle above boar & below head
- ringed pellet-triangle within ring above horse

*1 example in the CCI*
*Illustrated: dies 29/53*

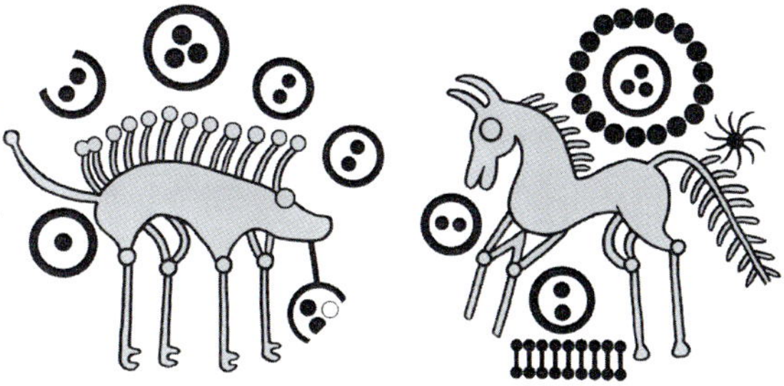

9b

BMC 3200

- pellet rosette above boar
- ringed pellet-triangle within ring above horse

*6 examples in the CCI*
*2 obverse dies, 2 reverse dies*
*Illustrated: dies 31/55*

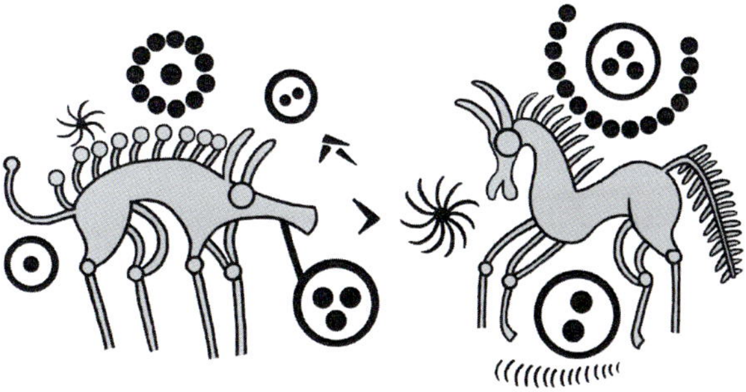

9c

- pellet ring above boar
- ringed double-pellet below boar
- ringed pellet-triangle within ring above horse

*1 example in the CCI*
*Illustrated: dies 32/56*

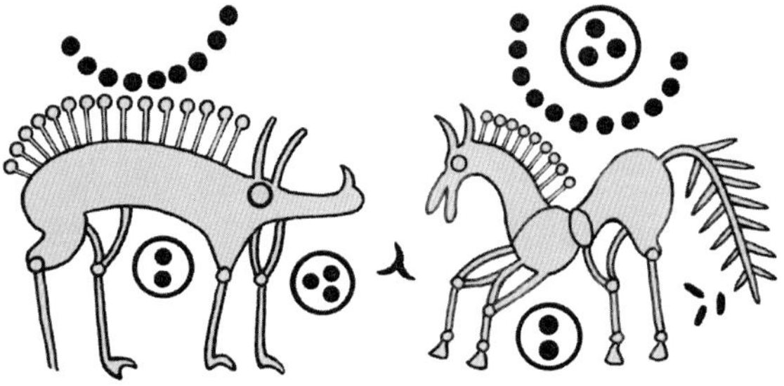

---

9d

- large ringed double-pellet within pellet ring above boar
- ringed pellet-triangle below horse

*1 example in the CCI*
*Illustrated: dies 33/57*

---

9e

- both forelegs of boar are bifurcated
- ringed pellet-triangle below boar & below horse

*2 examples in the CCI*
*1 obverse die, 2 reverse dies*
*Illustrated: dies 34/59*

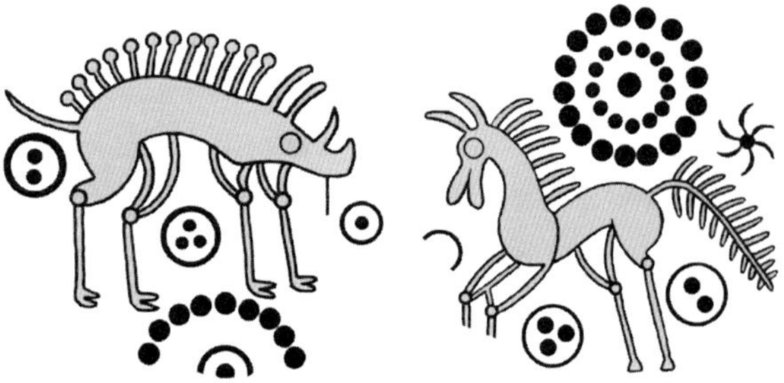

---

9f

- boar is a degraded version of 9b
- ringed pellet-triangle below horse

*1 example in the CCI*
*Illustrated: dies 35/60*

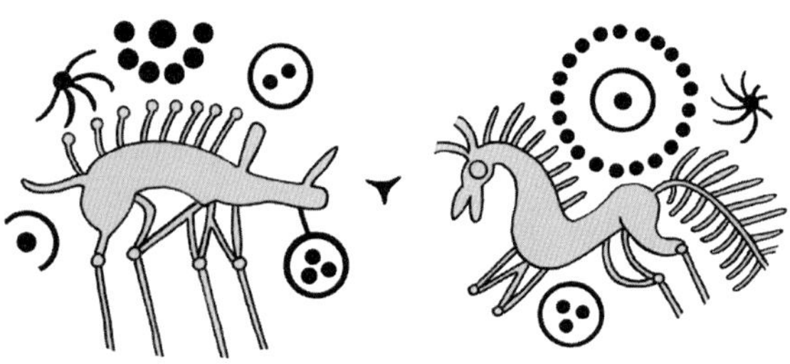

# Type 10 Two-Pellet Proto Boar

**Boar right with bifurcated left legs shown centrally between solid right legs.**

**Horse left with long fern tail.**

7. *The boar's forestal ferocity is emphasised by its exaggerated dorsal crest, the horse's virility (and fertility) by its long shaggy tail. Rich Type 10a, Two-Pellet Proto Boar.*

---

## 10a

- ringed double-pellets below boar & boar's head
- ringed double-pellet below horse

*3 examples in the CCI*
*1 obverse die, 1 reverse die*
*Illustrated: dies 36/61*

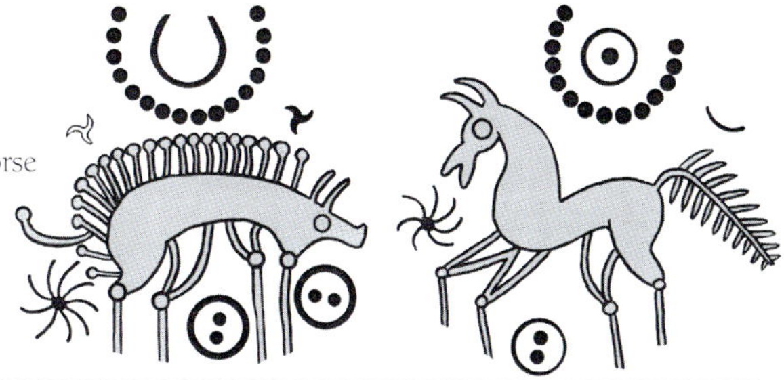

---

## 10b

- ringed double-pellets above boar's rump & below
- nothing below horse

*2 examples in the CCI*
*1 obverse die, 1 reverse die*
*Illustrated: dies 37/62*

## Type 11 Pin-Mane Proto Boar

**Boar right with bifurcated left legs shown centrally between solid right legs.**

**Horse left with short fern tail and pronounced pin mane.**

---

11a

- ringed triple-pellet below horse

*4 examples in the CCI*
*2 obverse dies, 3 reverse dies*
*Illustrated: dies 39/64*

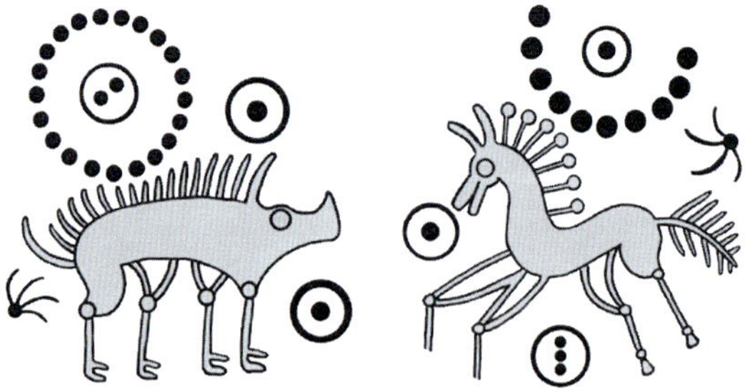

---

11b

BMC 3204

- 2 ringed pellets within pellet ring above horse, ringed pellet below

*2 examples in the CCI*
*2 obverse dies (1 from Type 11a)*
*1 reverse die*
*Illustrated: dies 39/66*

---

## Type 12 Spilsby Stag

**Boar right with bifurcated left legs shown centrally between solid right legs.**

**Horse left with short fern tail and a bar through the mane.**

---

12a

BMC 3203

- ringed double-pellet below horse

*7 examples in the CCI*
*2 obverse dies (1 from Type 11b)*
*2 reverse dies*
*Illustrated: dies 41/68*

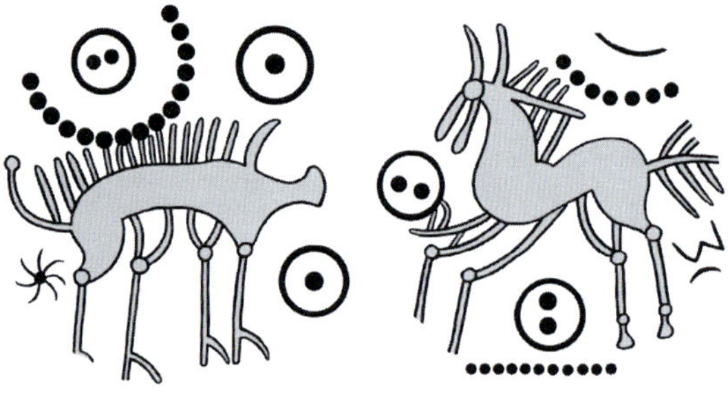

**12b**

- ringed pellet below horse

*2 examples in the CCI*
*2 obverse dies (1 from Type 12a)*
*2 reverse dies*
*Illustrated: dies 41/69*

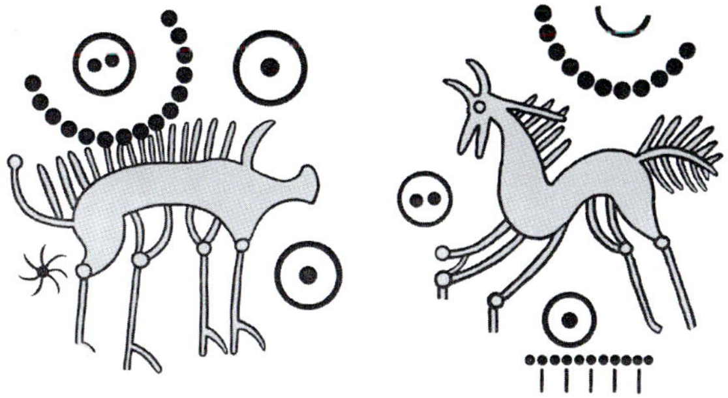

## Type 13 Triskele Proto Boar

**Boar right with bifurcated left legs shown centrally between solid right legs (with variation).**

**Horse left with long thin tail stranded on one side.**

**13a**

- triskele above & below horse

*10 examples in the CCI*
*3 obverse dies (1 from Type 12a)*
*2 reverse dies.*
*Illustrated: dies 43/71*

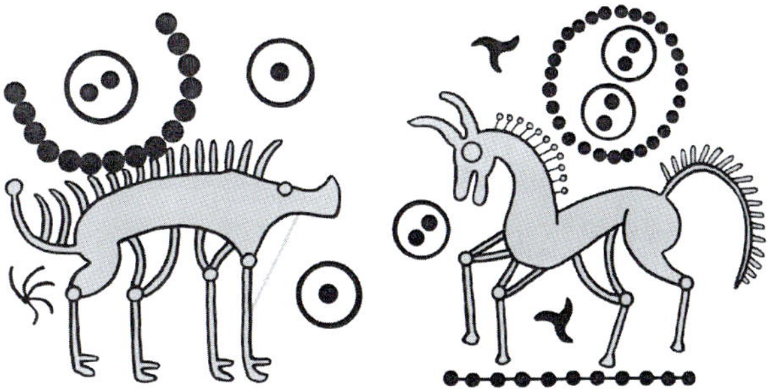

**13b**

- solar device above boar
- boar has solid right foreleg
- horse has solid left foreleg
- triskele below horse

*1 example in the CCI*
*obverse die from Type 13a*
*Illustrated: dies 44/73*

**8.** *Rich Type 13a. Note solid triskele above and below horse.*

**9.** *Rich Type 13b. Note triskele above and below boar and two expanded neck torcs under horse's tail.*

**10.** *Rich Type 18a. Why is the horse kneeling?*

## Type 14 Mercedes Proto Boar

**Boar right with bifurcated left legs shown centrally between solid right legs.**

**Horse left with short fern tail.**

---

14a

- ringed pellet below horse's head
- ringed concave triangle below

*2 examples in the CCI*
*1 obverse die, 1 reverse die*
*Illustrated: dies 45/74*

---

14b

- ringed double-pellet below horse's head
- ringed concave triangle below

*1 example in the CCI*
*Illustrated: dies 46/75*

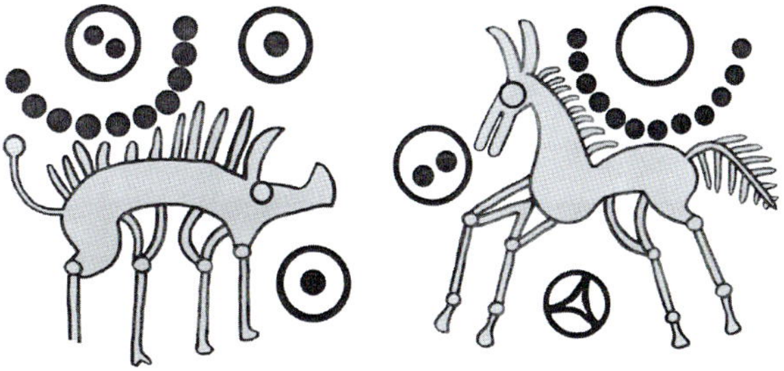

---

14c

- ringed pellet below horse's head
- Mercedes symbol below

*2 examples in the CCI*
*1 obverse die, 1 reverse die.*
*Illustrated: dies 47/76*

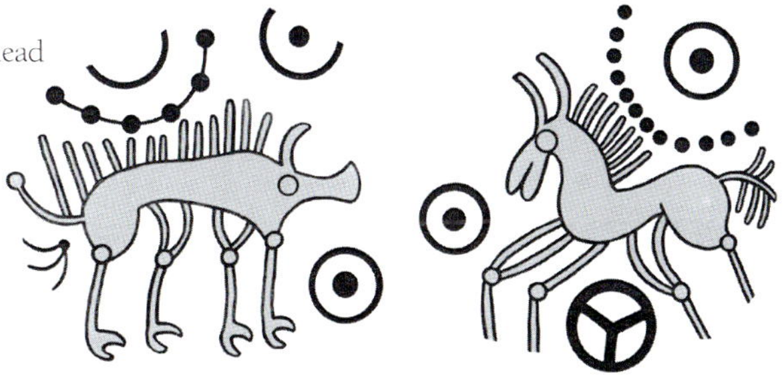

# Type 15 Evans Wheel Type

**Boar right with W shaped forelegs.**

**Horse right with long thin tail.**

---

15a

VA 860-1 BMC 3212

- spoked wheels behind & before boar
- spoked wheel above horse

*3 examples in the CCI*
*1 obverse die, 1 reverse die.*
*Illustrated: dies 48/77*

---

15b

ABC 1791

- 2 pellet-triangles above boar
- spiral below boar
- spoked wheel above horse
- ringed double-pellet below horse

*1 example in the CCI*
*Illustrated: dies 49/78*

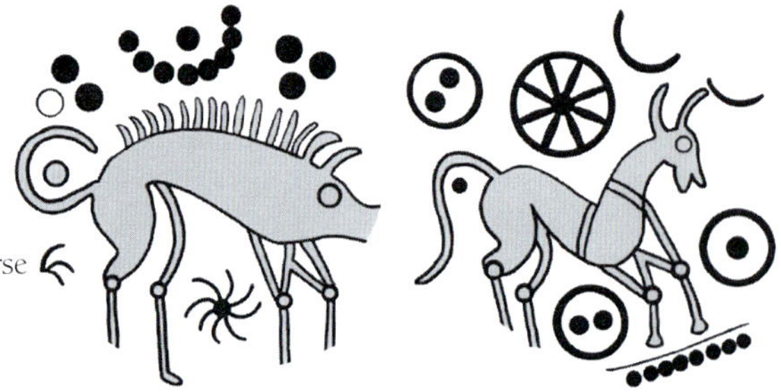

---

# Type 16 W-Forelegs Proto Boar

**Boar right with W shaped forelegs.**

**Horse left with long thin tail.**

---

16a

VA 857-5 BMC 3208-3209

- 3 ringed pellets around boar
- ringed pellets below horse's head & below

*46 examples in the CCI*
*4 obverse dies (1 from Type 10b), 10 reverse dies.*
*Illustrated: dies 51/83*

## 16b

**BMC 3199, 3210-3211**

- as 16a but additional ringed pellet above horse's tail

*33 examples in the CCI*
*2 obverse dies (1 from Type 16a)*
*6 reverse dies*
*Illustrated: dies 53/90*

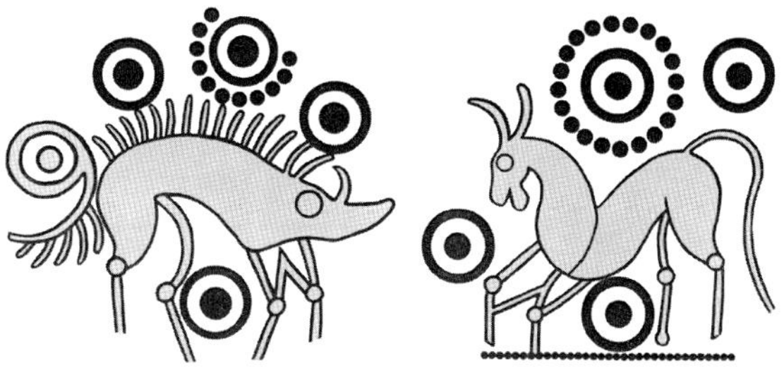

---

## 16c

- ringed pellets above boar's rump & below
- ringed pellets above horse's head & below

*2 examples in the CCI*
*1 obverse die, 1 reverse die.*
*Illustrated: dies 54/95*

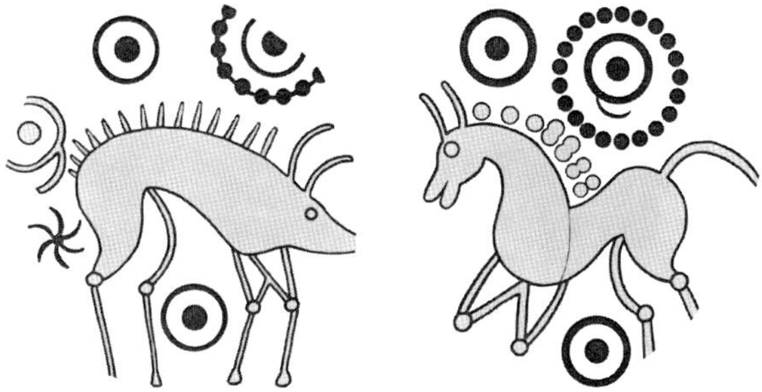

---

## 16d

- ringed pellets above boar's head & below
- ringed pellets below horse's head & below

*5 examples in the CCI*
*1 obverse die, 1 reverse die*
*Illustrated: dies 55/96*

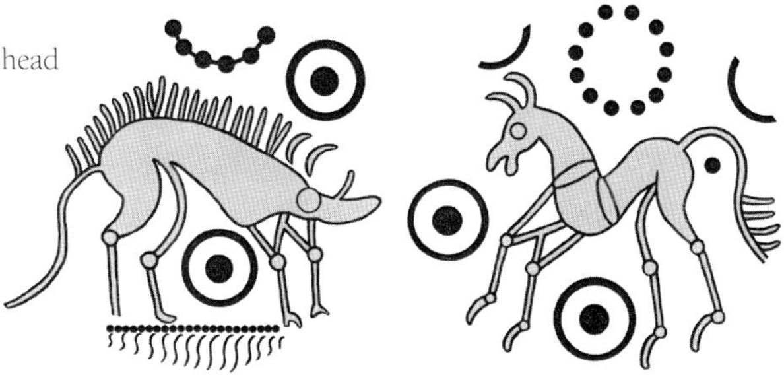

---

## 16e

- boar transitional type from W to Y forelegs
- rings below horse's head & below

*1 example in the CCI*
*Illustrated: dies 56/97*

## Type 17 Two-Ring Proto Boar

**Pierced boar right with W shaped forelegs.**

**Horse left with long thin tail.**

---

17a

BMC 3198

- large pellet rings above & below boar
- kneeling horse
- 4 ringed pellets around horse

*3 examples in the CCI*
*2 obverse dies, 1 reverse die*
*Illustrated: dies 58/98*

---

17b

- large pellet rings above & below boar
- kneeling horse
- ringed pellet before horse

*1 example in the CCI*
*obverse die from Type 17a*
*Illustrated: dies 58/99*

---

## Type 18 One-Leg Proto Boar

**Boar right with Y shaped forelegs.**

**Horse left with long thin tail.**

---

18a

ABC 1797

- boar has elaborate tail
- kneeling horse
- pellet below horse's tail

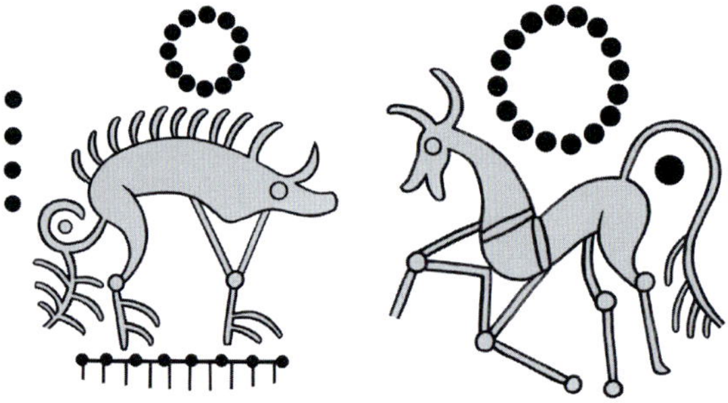

*7 examples in the CCI*
*1 obverse die, 2 reverse dies*
*Illustrated: dies 59/100*

### 18b

- star below boar's head
- kneeling horse
- pellet-triangle below horse's head, pellet below tail

*1 example in the CCI*
*Illustrated: dies 60/102*

## Type 19 Ladder-Mane Proto Boar

**Boar right with Y shaped forelegs.**

**Horse left with thin tail and ladder mane.**

### 19a

- star below boar's head
- kneeling horse
- concave triangle before horse
- spoked wheel above horse

*1 example in the CCI*
*obverse die from Type 18b*
*Illustrated: dies 60/103*

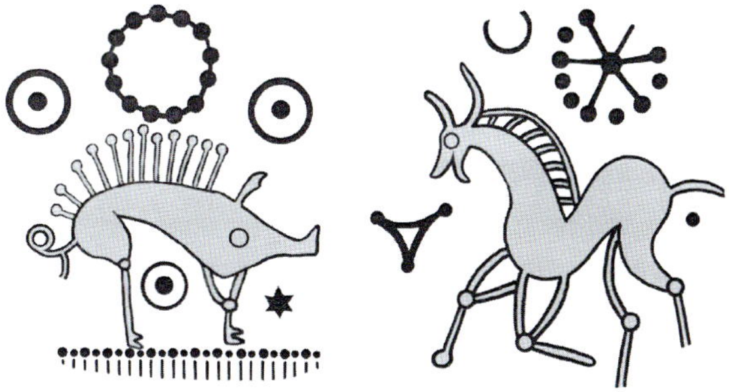

### 19b

- ring below boar's head
- kneeling horse
- pellet-triangle before horse
- spoked wheel above horse

*2 examples in the CCI*
*1 obverse die, 2 reverse dies.*
*Illustrated: dies 61/104*

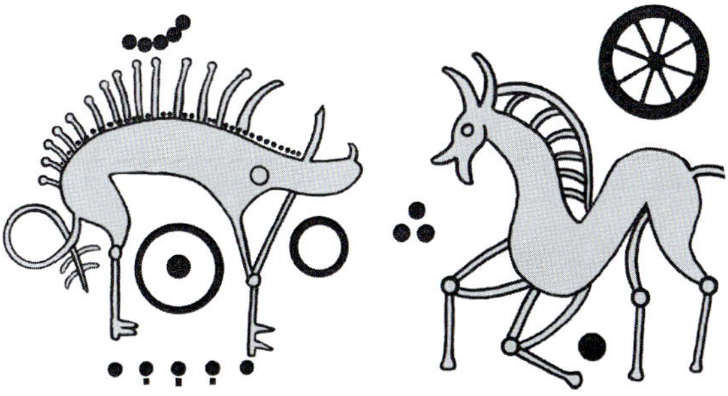

## Type 20 Comb-Bristle Proto Boar

**Boar right with Y shaped forelegs.**

**Horse right with thin tail.**

---

Type 20

- boar has ladder bristles
- double-ring below boar
- double-ring above horse

*2 examples in the CCI*
*2 obverse dies, 2 reverse dies*
*Illustrated: dies 63/107*

---

## Type 21 Y Leg, Horse Left

**Boar right with Y shaped forelegs.**

**Horse left with long thin tail.**

---

21a

VA 857-3 BMC 3207

- 4 ringed pellets around boar
- kneeling horse
- pellet below horse's tail

*3 examples in the CCI*
*2 obverse dies, 1 reverse die.*
*Illustrated: dies 65/108*

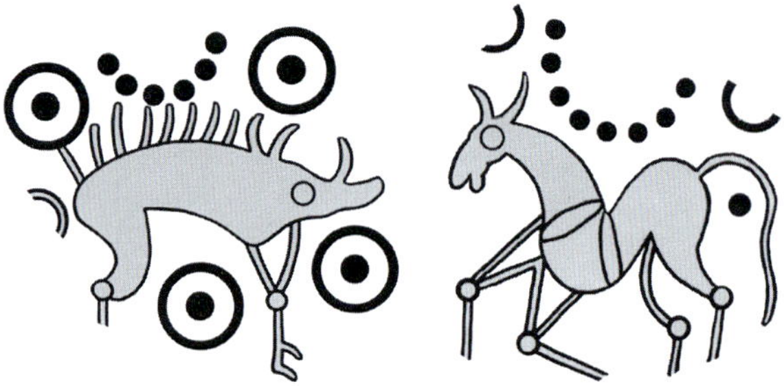

---

21b

VA 857-1

- 4 ringed pellets around boar
- 4 ringed pellets around horse
- pellet below horse's tail

*5 examples in the CCI*
*2 obverse dies, 4 reverse dies*
*Illustrated: dies 66/110*

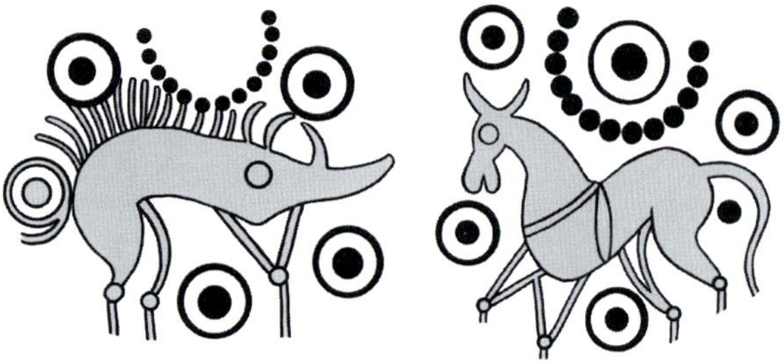

21c

- 4 ringed pellets around boar
- ringed pellet below horse
- torc below horse's tail

*2 examples in the CCI*
*1 obverse die, 1 reverse die*
*Illustrated: dies 68/113*

21d

ABC 1794

- 4 ringed pellets around boar
- 3 ringed pellets around horse
- spoked wheel above horse
- pellet below horse's tail

*4 examples in the CCI*
*1 obverse die, 3 reverse dies*
*Illustrated: dies 69/114*

## Type 22 South Ferriby Boar

**Boar right with Y shaped forelegs.**

**Horse right with long thin tail.**

22a

ABC 1800 VA 875-1, 875-2

BMC 3214 - 3215

- pellet rosette above boar
- pellet ring above horse
- 3 ringed pellets around horse

*37 examples in the CCI*
*9 obverse dies, 9 reverse dies*
*Illustrated: dies 70/118*

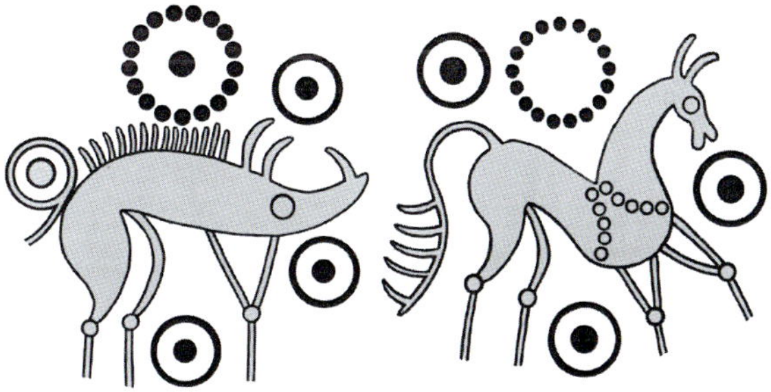

22b

- semi elevated boar's tail
- 2 pellets in pellet ring above boar
- 3 ringed pellets around boar
- 2 pellets in pellet ring above horse
- 3 ringed pellets around horse

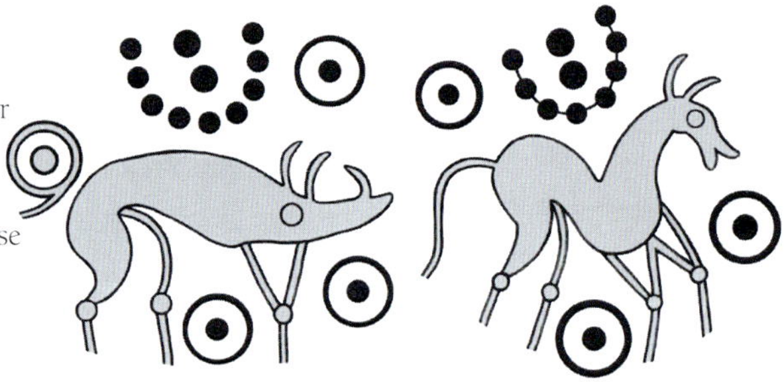

*39 examples in the CCI*
*15 obverse dies, 16 reverse dies.*
*Illustrated: dies 89/137*

---

22c

- elongated boar & horse
- fully elevated boar's tail
- 2 pellets in pellet ring above boar
- 2 pellets in pellet ring above horse
- ringed pellet below horse

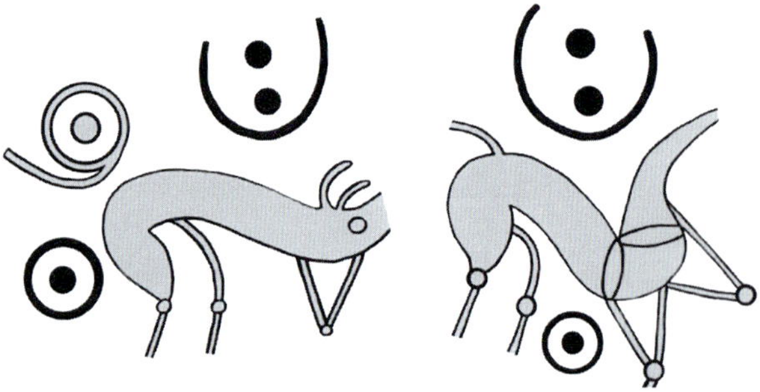

*11 examples in the CCI*
*2 obverse dies, 2 reverse dies*
*Illustrated: dies 94/142*

---

## Type 23 Y-Leg Boar Left

**Boar left with Y shaped forelegs.**

**Horse left with thin tail.**

---

Type 23

- elongated boar faces left
- pellet-triangle below horse's tail
- ringed pellet below horse

*1 example in the CCI*
*Illustrated: dies 96/144*

## Type 24 South Ferriby Shrimp

**Shrimplike boar right with Y shaped forelegs.**

**Horse right with thin tail.**

---

24a

- 4 rings around boar
- ring below horse

*3 examples in the CCI*
*1 obverse die, 1 reverse die*
*Illustrated: dies 97/145*

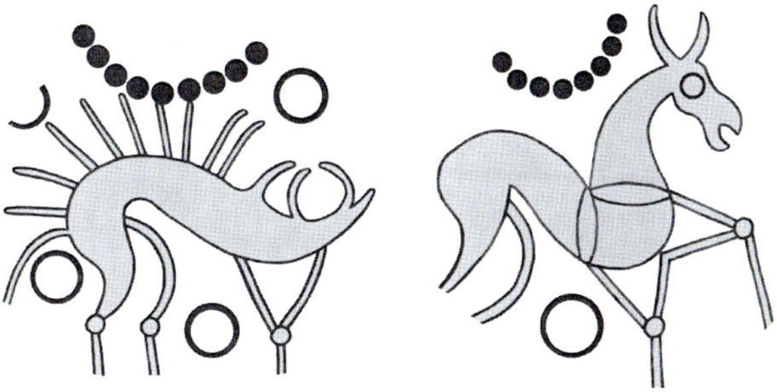

---

24b

- ring above boar's rump
- ring below boar
- ring below horse's tail
- ringed pellet below horse

*2 examples in the CCI*
*1 obverse die, 1 reverse die.*
*Illustrated: dies 98/146*

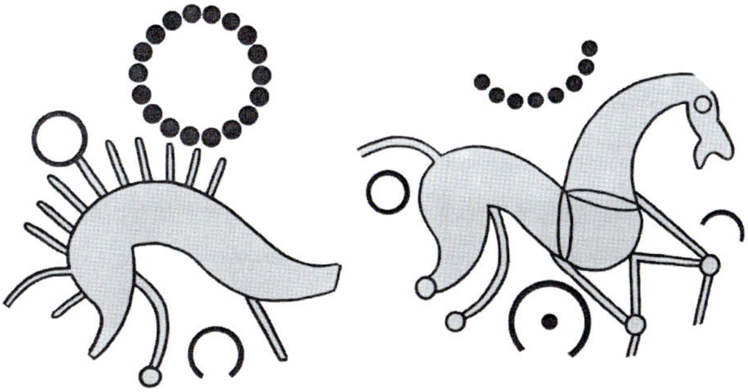

---

24c

- ring above boar's head & below
- pellet below boar's tail
- pellet below horse's tail
- ring below horse

*6 examples in the CCI*
*3 obverse dies, 3 reverse dies*
*Illustrated: dies 101/149*

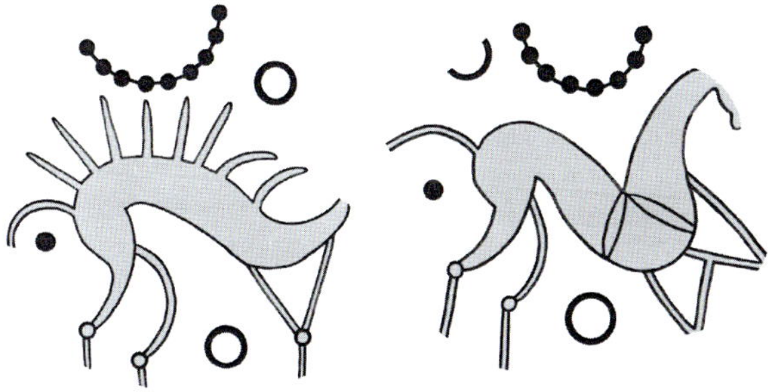

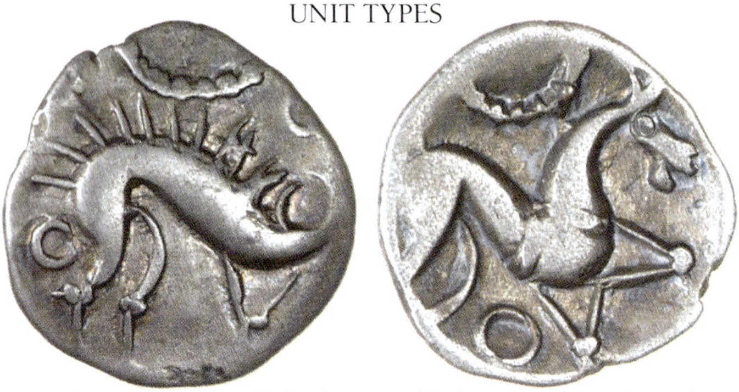

**11.** *Rich Type 24a. Note shrimplike boar has Y-shaped forelegs and horse has W-form forelegs.*

## 24d

**BMC 3218**

- pellet below boar's tail
- ring below boar
- pellet below horse's tail

*38 examples in the CCI*
*8 obverse dies, 7 reverse dies*
*Illustrated: dies 102/150*

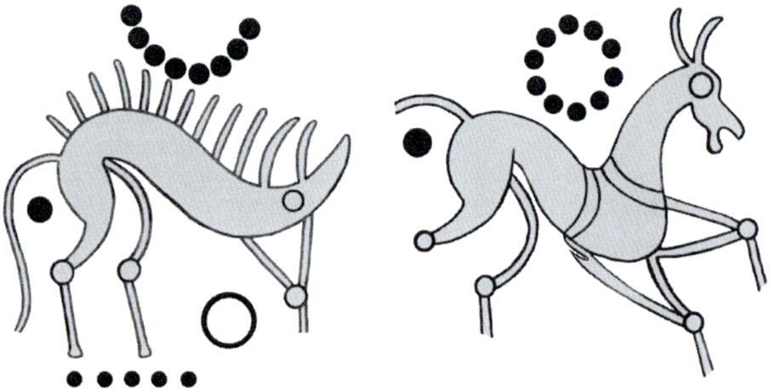

---

## 24e

**ABC 1803 VA 877-1, 877-7**

**BMC 3219-3227**

- pellet below boar's tail
- pellet below horse's tail

*9 examples in the CCI*
*18 obverse dies, 29 reverse dies*
*Illustrated: dies 110/159*

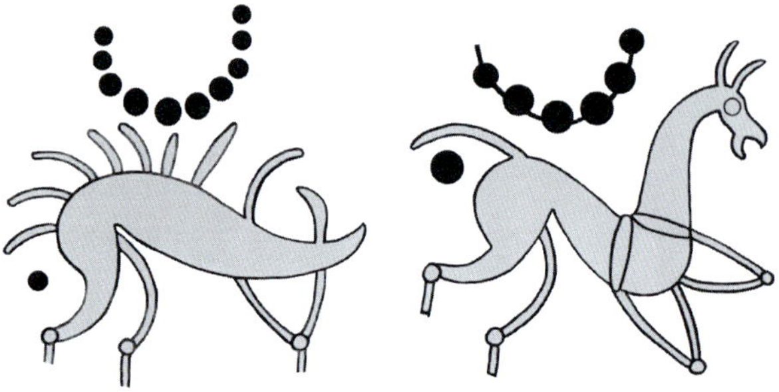

---

## 24f

- nothing around boar or horse

*6 examples in the CCI*
*3 obverse dies (1 from Type 18a)*
*2 reverse dies*
*Illustrated: dies 127/186*

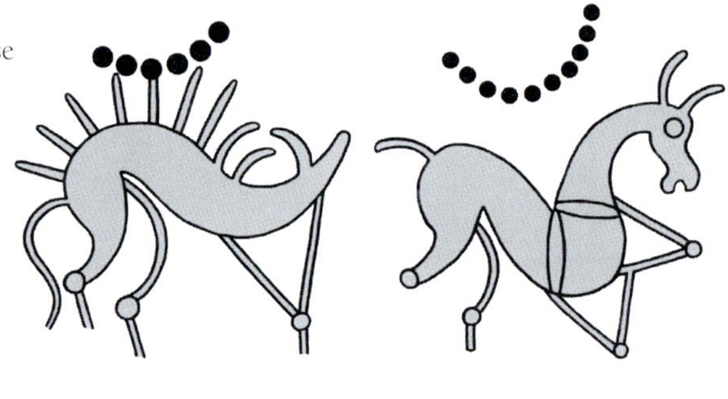

# Type 25 South Ferriby Dashed Mane

**Boar right with Y shaped forelegs.**

**Horse right with thin tail and dashed mane.**

---

25a

BMC 3216

- pellet-triangle above boar's head
- ringed pellet below boar
- pellet-triangle below horse

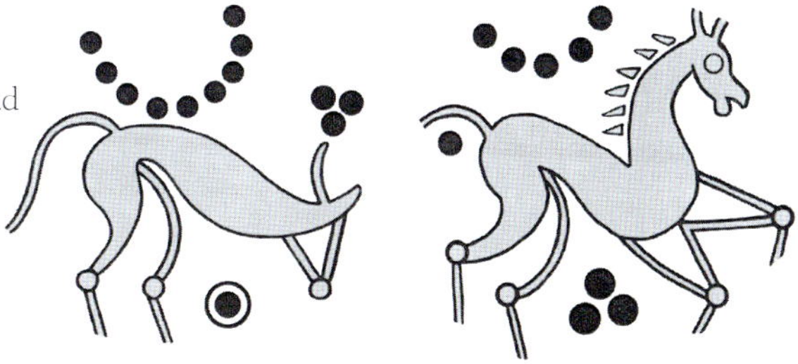

*2 examples in the CCI*
*1 obverse die, 1 reverse die.*
*Illustrated: dies 129/188*

---

25b

- partly obliterated boar

ringed pellet below horse

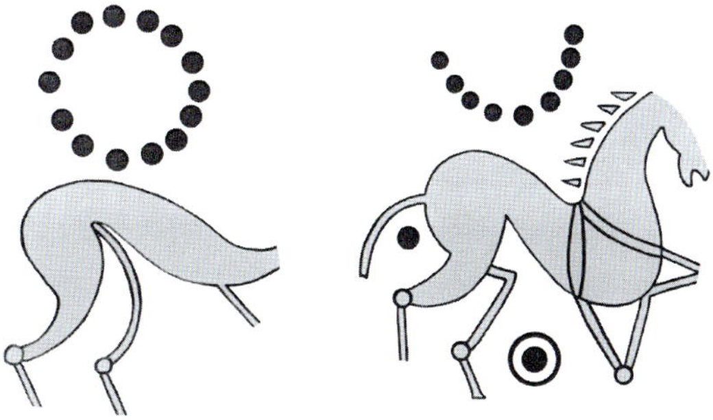

*1 example in the CCI*
*obverse die from Type 25a*
*Illustrated: dies 129/189*

---

25c

VA 877-5

- partly obliterated boar
- large ringed pellet above horse
- pellet above head

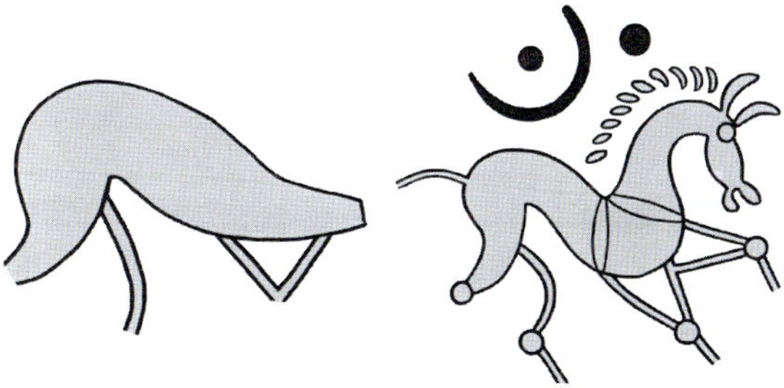

*4 examples in the CCI*
*obliterated obverse, 2 reverse dies*
*Illustrated: reverse die 190*

## Type 26 South Ferriby Natural Head Right

**Obliterated obverse.**

**Horse right with natural head, pellet rosette above.**

26a

- nothing around the horse

*12 examples in the CCI*
*5 reverse dies.*
*Illustrated: reverse die 192*

26b

- pellet below tail

*8 examples in the CCI*
*4 reverse dies.*
*Illustrated: reverse die 200*

26c

- pellet below tail & below

*1 example in the CCI*
*Illustrated: reverse die 201*

26d

VA 877-3

BMC 3230-3232

- pellet-triangle below tail

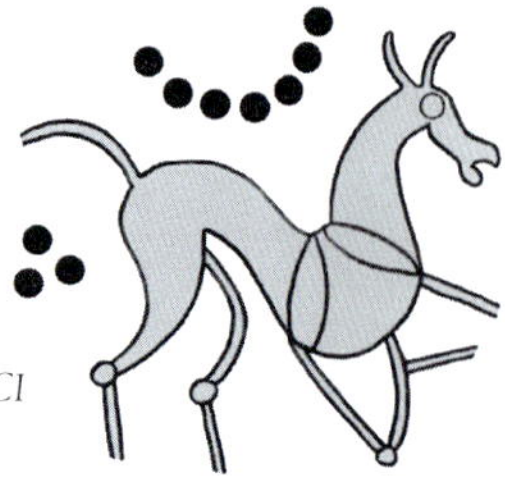

*10 examples in the CCI*
*6 reverse dies.*
*Illustrated: reverse die 202*

26e

BMC 3217

- pellet-triangle below

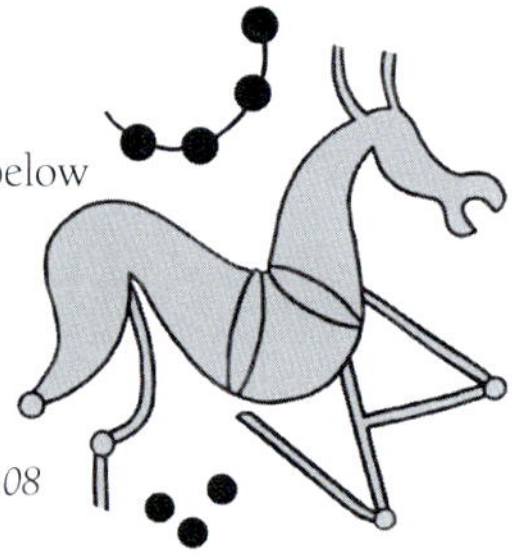

*6 examples in the CCI*
*2 reverse dies.*
*Illustrated: reverse die 208*

26f

- pellet-triangle below head

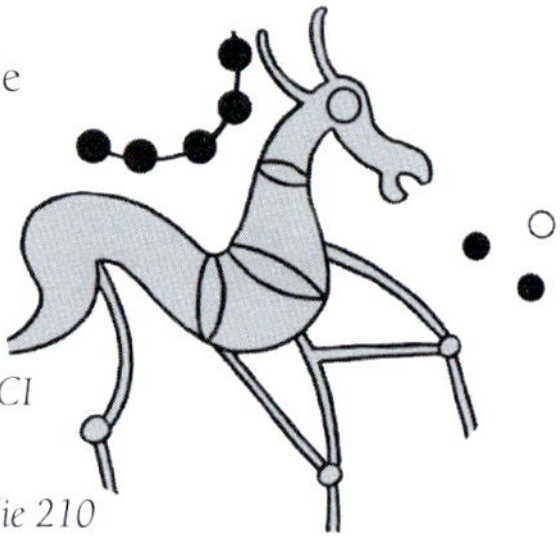

*6 examples in the CCI*
*1 reverse die.*
*Illustrated: reverse die 210*

26g

- pellet-triangle below head
- pellet-triangle below

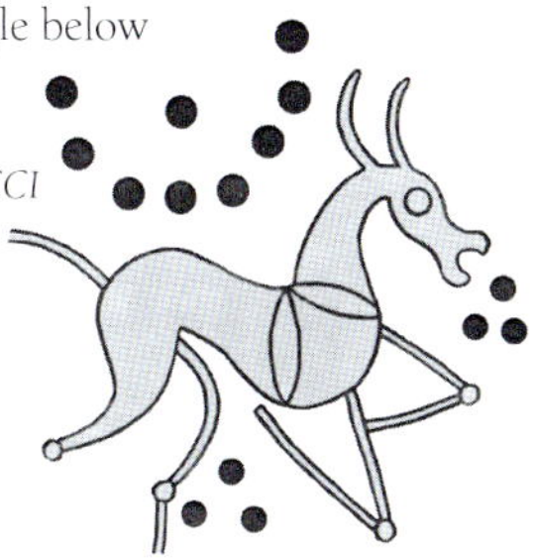

*8 examples in the CCI*
*1 reverse die.*
*Illustrated: reverse die 211*

26h

- pellet-triangle below tail
- pellet-triangle below head
- pellet-triangle below

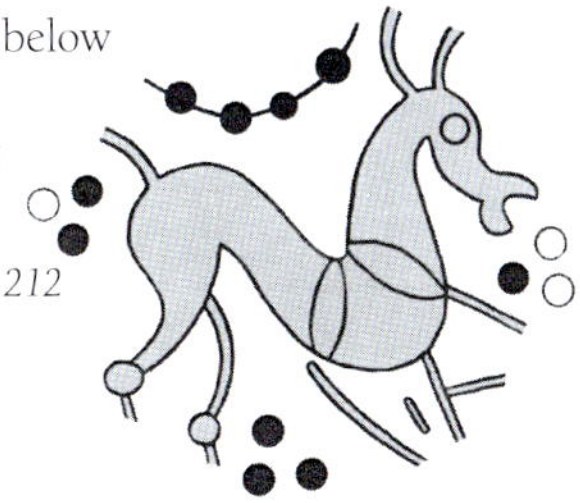

*2 examples in the CCI*
*1 reverse die.*
*Illustrated: reverse die 212*

## Type 27 South Ferriby Natural Head Left

**Obliterated obverse.**

**Horse left with natural head, pellet rosette above.**

27a

- pellet below tail
- pellet below

*1 example in the CCI*
*Illustrated: reverse die 213*

27b

VA 887-1

- ringed pellet above tail
- pellet below tail
- pellet-triangle below

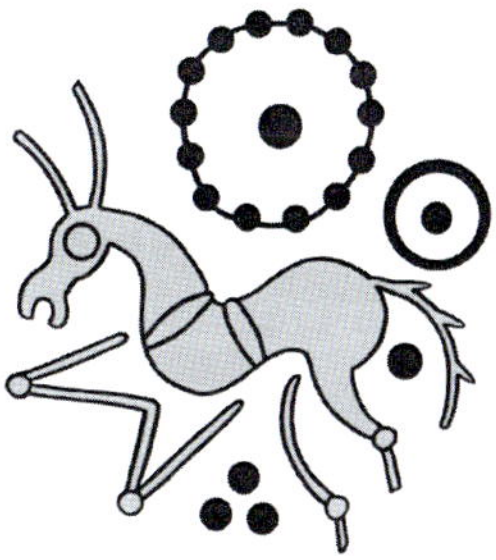

*14 examples in the CCI*
*4 reverse dies.*
*Illustrated: reverse die 214*

27c

ABC 1809

- pellet-triangle below tail
- pellet-triangle below

*6 examples in the CCI*
*2 reverse dies.*
*Illustrated: reverse die 218*

## Type 28 South Ferriby Stork Head Right

**Obliterated obverse.**

**Horse right with stork head, pellet rosette above.**

28a

ABC 1806

VA 884-1

BMC 3228-3229

- pellet below tail

*62 examples in the CCI*

*18 reverse dies.*

*Illustrated: reverse die 226*

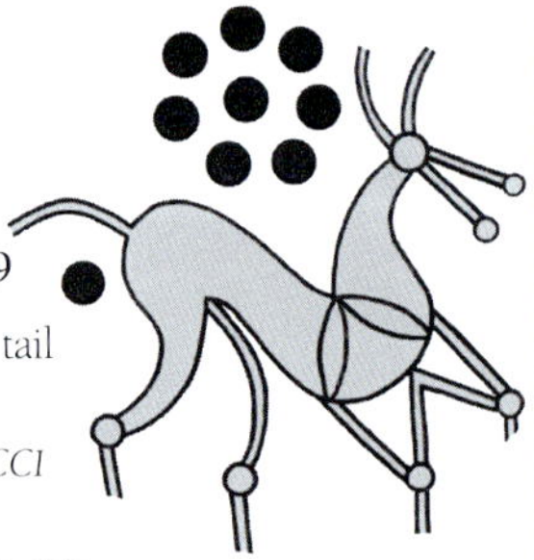

28b

- pellet-triangle below tail

*2 examples in the CCI*

*1 reverse die.*

*Illustrated: reverse die 241*

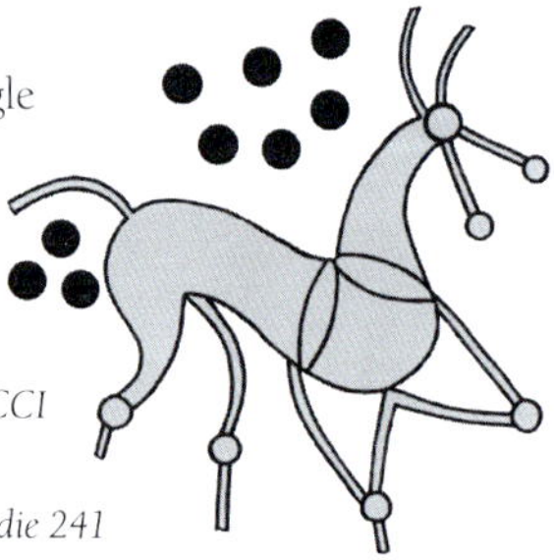

28c

- pellet-cross below

*1 example in the CCI*

*Illustrated: reverse die 242*

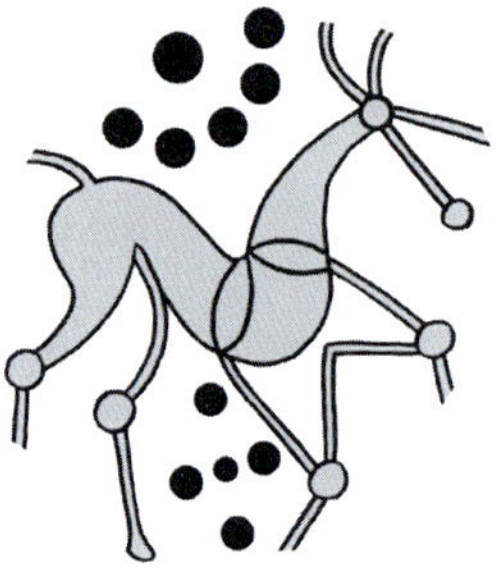

## Type 29 South Ferriby Stork Head Left

**Obliterated obverse.**

**Horse left with stork head, pellet rosette above.**

29

- pellet-triangle below tail

*2 examples in the CCI*

*2 reverse dies.*

*Illustrated: reverse die 221*

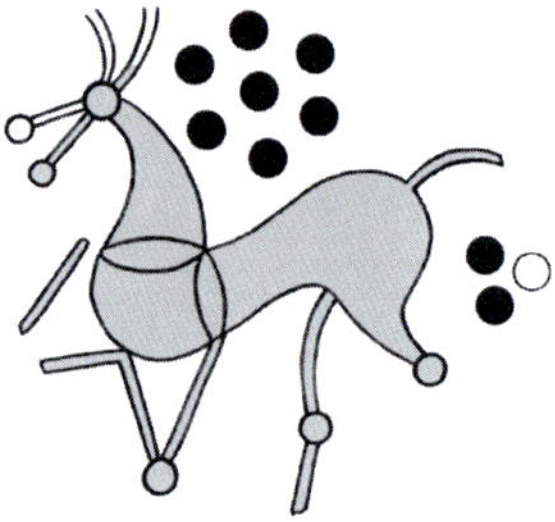

## Type 30 South Ferriby Cross

**Obliterated obverse.**

**Horse left with triangular head, pellet rosette above.**

30

ABC 1812 BMC 3234

- cross below with pellets in the angles

*2 examples in the CCI*
*1 reverse die.*
*Illustrated: reverse die 220*

## Type 31 South Ferriby Domino

**Obliterated obverse.**

**Horse right with stork head, 'domino' above.**

31

ABC 1815 BMC 3233

- 'domino' contains 4 pellets

*4 examples in the CCI*
*3 reverse dies.*
*Illustrated: reverse die 243*

12. *The 'domino' motif also occurs on a Corieltavian gold stater (ABC 1758) and occasionally looks more like a crown. The ancient Egyptian symbol for earth is a row of dots in a thin rectangle. Might 'domino' dots have a similar meaning? This Domino stater was found near Hull, E.Yorks., 23 July 2011.*

## Type 32 South Ferriby Kite

**Obliterated obverse.**

**Horse left, 'kite' above.**

32a

ABC 1818

- 'kite' contains 1 pellet

*2 examples in the CCI*
*1 reverse die.*
*Illustrated: reverse die 246*

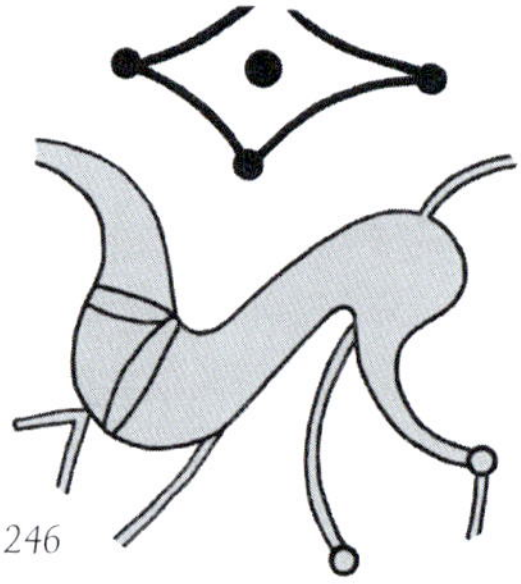

32b

- 'kite' contains 4 pellets
- pellet-triangle below tail

*4 examples in the CCI*
*1 reverse die.*
*Illustrated: reverse die 247*

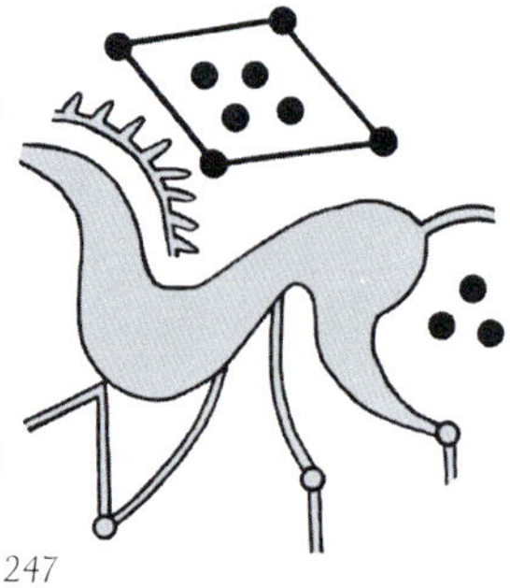

13. *The 'kite' motif also occurs on a Corieltavian gold stater (ABC 1761) and silver coins of the Iceni (ABC 1549-57). Found near Sleaford, Lincs., this Kite stater shows a lunate horse with multiple ears.*

# Catalogue of half unit types

## Type 33 Decorated Boar Right

**Boar right with Y shaped forelegs.**

**Horse left.**

### 33a

ABC 1824 BMC 3236

- elaborate boar surrounded by ringed pellets & 'bear paws'
- wheel above horse
- 8 pointed star below horse

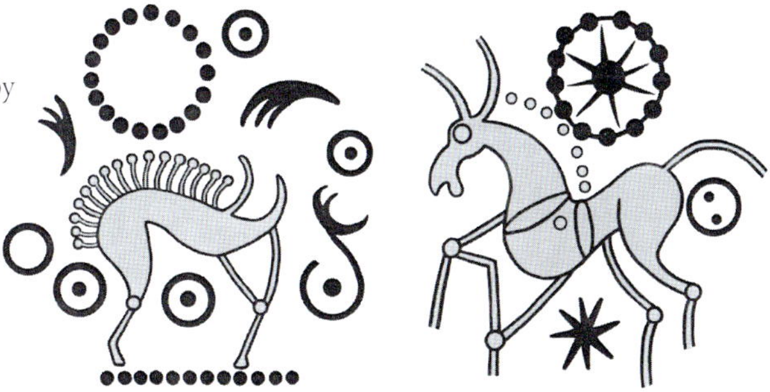

*10 examples in the CCI*
*1 obverse die, 4 reverse dies.*
*Illustrated: dies 130/248*

### 33b

BMC 3237

- as 33a but ring below horse

*2 examples in the CCI*
*1 obverse die (from Type 33a)*
*1 reverse die*
*Illustrated: dies 130/252*

### 33c

- boar partly obliterated
- wheel above horse
- nothing below horse

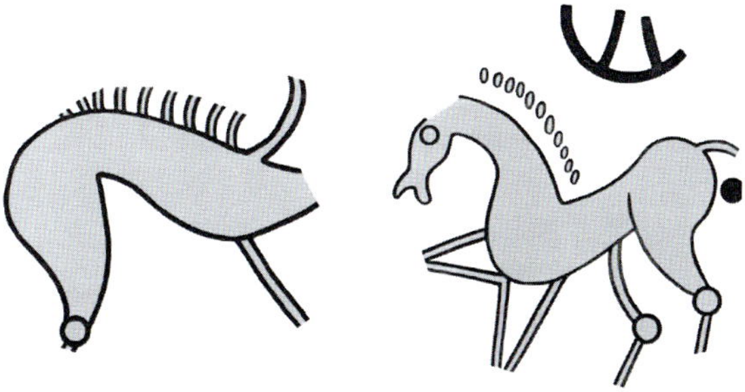

*1 example in the CCI*
*obverse die from Type 33a*
*Illustrated: dies 130/253*

33d

- boar partly or wholly obliterated
- 3 rings below boar, 1 before
- ring below horse

*4 examples in the CCI*
*1 obverse die, 1 reverse die*
*Illustrated: dies 131/254*

---

## Type 34 Decorated Boar Left

**Boar left with Y shaped forelegs.**

**Horse left.**

---

34a

BMC 3238-3239

- elaborate boar surrounded by
- ringed pellets, wheel above
- horse with hooked right rear leg
- pellet below horse's tail

*19 examples in the CCI*
*1 obverse die, 3 reverse dies.*
*Illustrated: dies 132/255*

---

34b

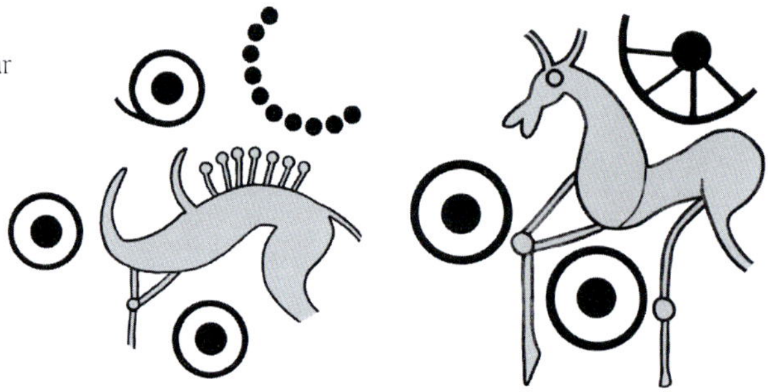

- 3 ringed pellets around boar
- wheel above horse
- ringed pellets below horse's head & below

*2 examples in the CCI*
*2 obverse dies, 1 reverse die*
*Illustrated: dies 133/258*

34c

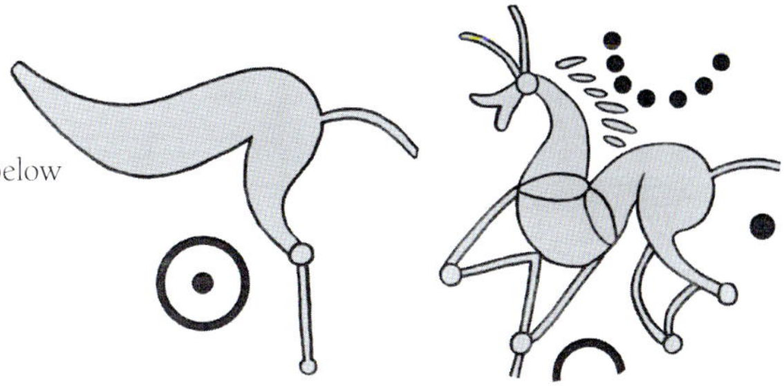

- boar partly obliterated
- pellet below horse's tail ring below

*3 examples in the CCI*
*1 obverse die, 1 reverse die*
*Illustrated: dies 135/259*

## Type 35 Double Wheel Type

**Boar right with Y shaped forelegs, 4 spoked wheel above.**

**Horse right, 4 spoked wheel above.**

35a

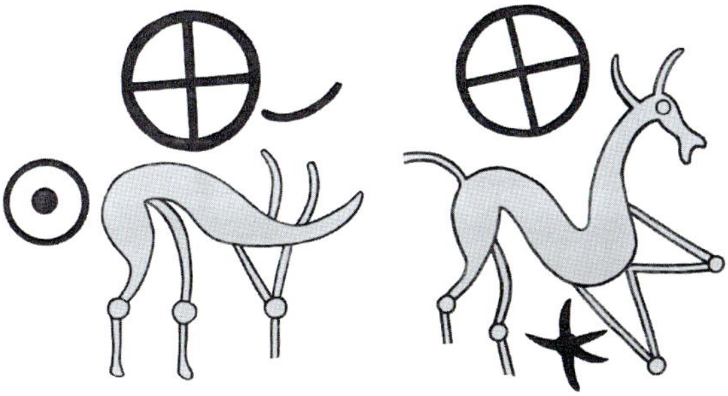

VA 862-1 BMC 3244-3245

- ringed pellet behind boar
- 5 pointed star below horse

*5 examples in the CCI*
*1 obverse die, 1 reverse die*
*Illustrated: dies 136/260*

35b

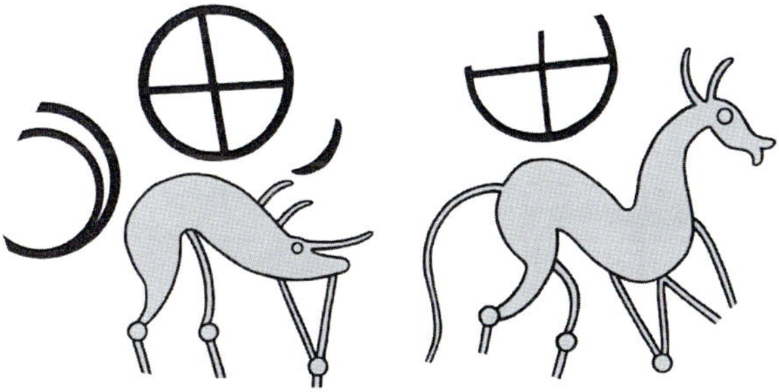

ABC 1827

- large ring (tail) behind boar
- nothing below horse

*7 examples in the CCI*
*2 obverse dies, 2 reverse dies*
*Illustrated: dies 137/261*

## Type 36 Transitional Half

**Boar right with Y shaped forelegs.**

**Horse right.**

---

36a

- wheel above boar
- wheel below boar's head
- pellet below horse's tail

*1 example in the CCI*
*Illustrated: dies 139/263*

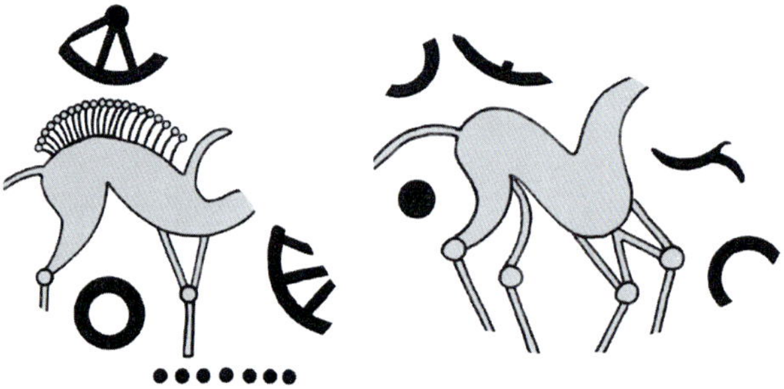

---

36b

- boar with very long bristles
- pellet below boar's tail
- pellet below horse's tail

*3 examples in the CCI*
*1 obverse die, 1 reverse die*
*Illustrated: dies 140/264*

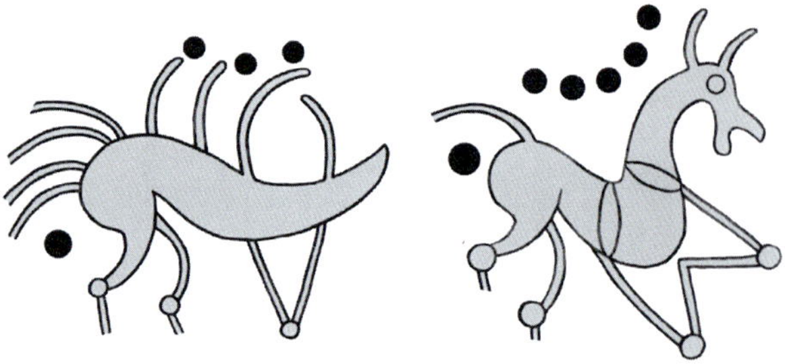

---

## Type 37 Natural Head Left

**Obliterated obverse.**

**Horse left with natural head, pellet rosette above.**

---

37a

BMC 3241-3243

- pellet below tail

*33 examples in the CCI*
*8 reverse dies.*
*Illustrated: reverse die 266*

37b

BMC 3240

- pellet-triangle below tail

*16 examples in the CCI*
*4 reverse dies.*
*Illustrated: reverse die 273*

**37c**

- pellet below tail & below

*3 examples in the CCI*
*2 reverse dies*
*Illustrated: reverse die 278*

**37d**

- pellet between forelegs
- pellet-triangle below

*10 examples in the CCI*
*4 reverse dies.*
*Illustrated: reverse die 280*

**37e**

- pellet between forelegs
- pellet below tail

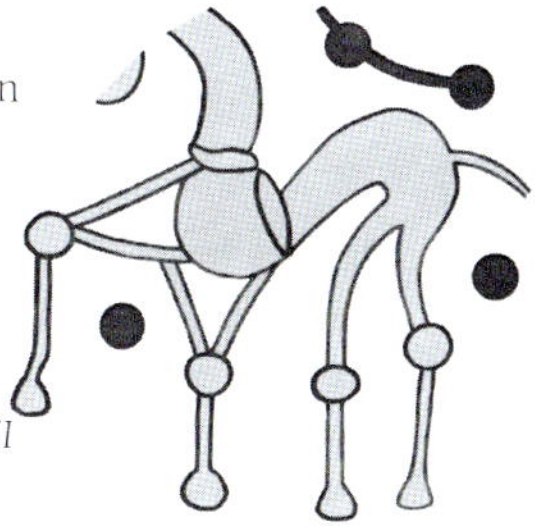

*3 examples in the CCI*
*2 reverse dies.*
*Illustrated: reverse die 283*

## Type 38 Stork Head Right

**Obliterated obverse.**

**Horse right with stork head, pellet rosette above.**

**38a**

- nothing around horse

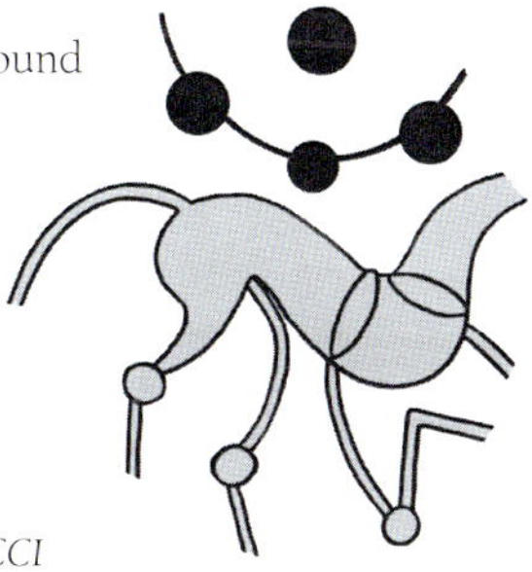

*1 example in the CCI*
*Illustrated: reverse die 285*

**38b**

- pellet below tail

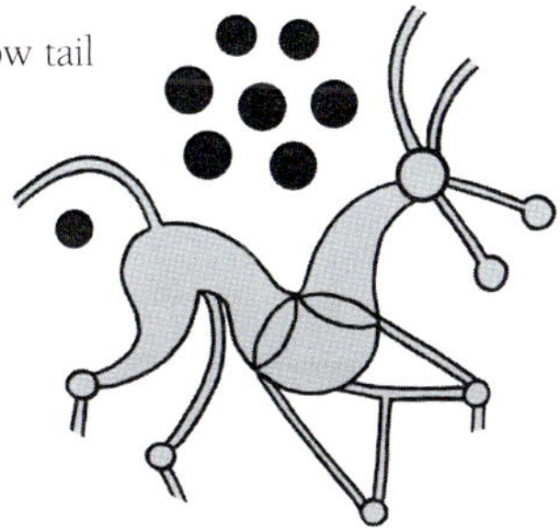

*20 examples in the CCI*
*7 reverse dies.*
*Illustrated: reverse die 286*

### 38c

- pellet below tail
- pellet between forelgs
- ringed pellet below

*2 examples in the CCI*
*1 reverse die*
*Illustrated: reverse die 293*

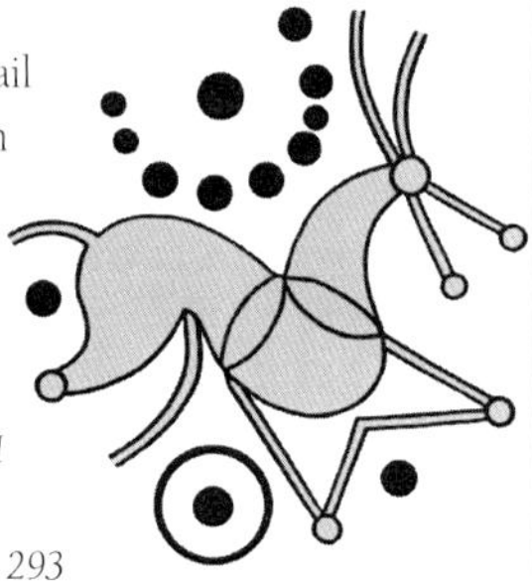

### 38d

- pellet below tail
- pellet-triangle below

*5 examples in the CCI*
*3 reverse dies.*
*Illustrated: reverse die 294*

### 38e

- as 38d but ringed pellet in centre of rosette

*2 examples in the CCI*
*1 reverse die.*
*Illustrated: reverse die 297*

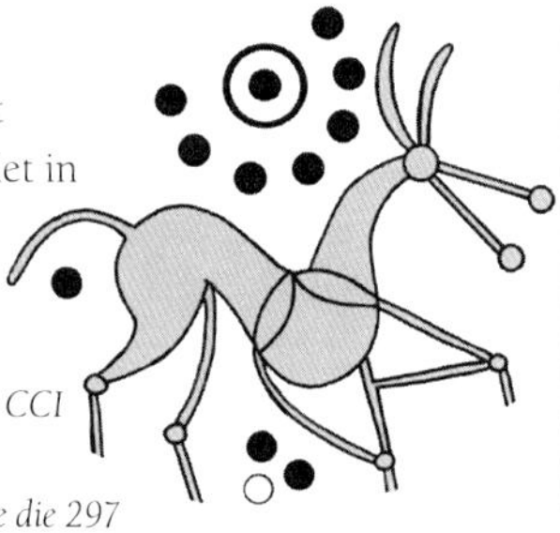

### 38f

BMC 3251-3253, 3255

- pellet-triangle below tail

*19 examples in the CCI*
*7 reverse dies.*
*Illustrated: reverse die 298*

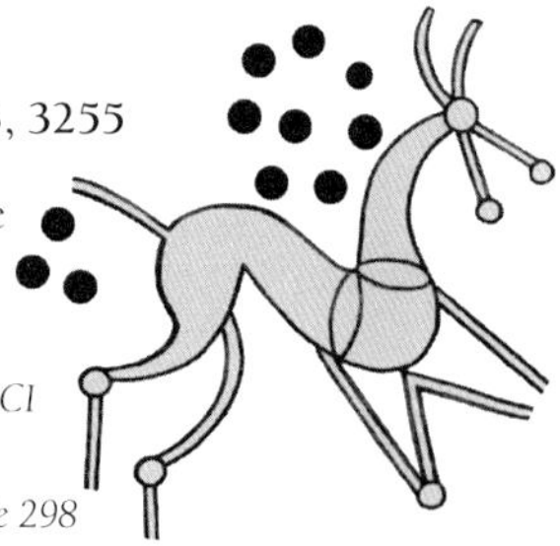

### 38g

ABC 1833

- pellet above & below muzzle
- pellet-triangle below tail

*5 examples in the CCI*
*2 reverse dies.*
*Illustrated: reverse die 305*

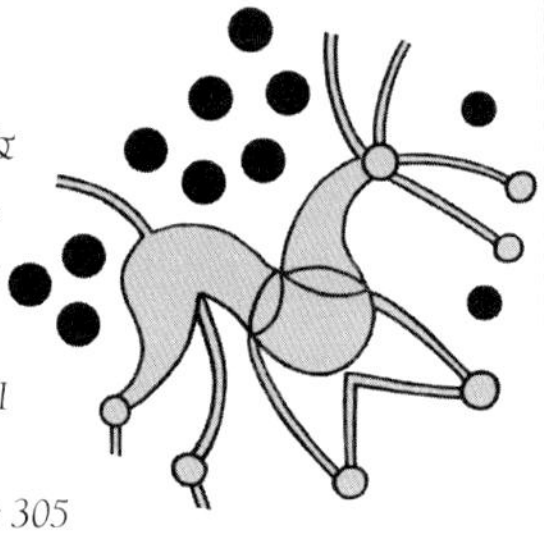

### 38h

VA 879-1 BMC 3254

- pellet triangle below tail
- pellet-triangle below

*25 examples in the CCI*
*13 reverse dies.*
*Illustrated: reverse die 308*

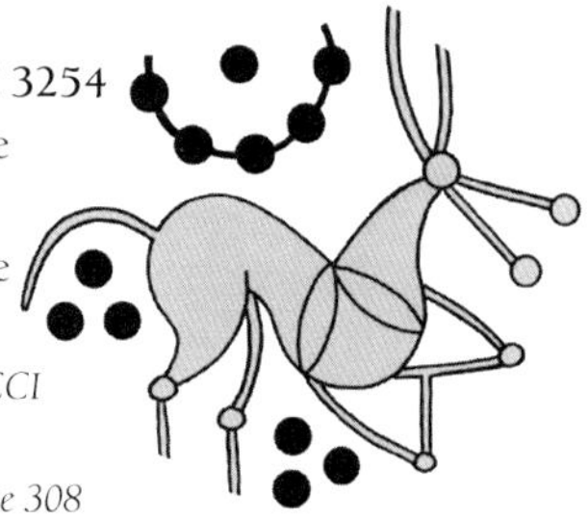

### 38i

- pellet triangle above
- pellet-triangle below tail

*1 example in the CCI*
*Illustrated: reverse die 320*

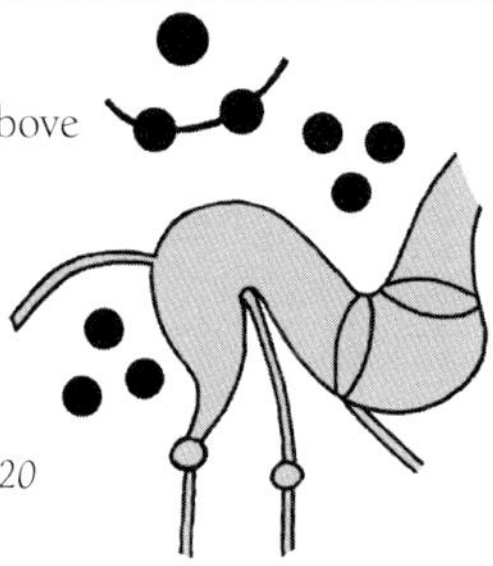

### 38j

- pellet triangle below tail
- pellet below

*1 example in the CCI*
*Illustrated: reverse die 321*

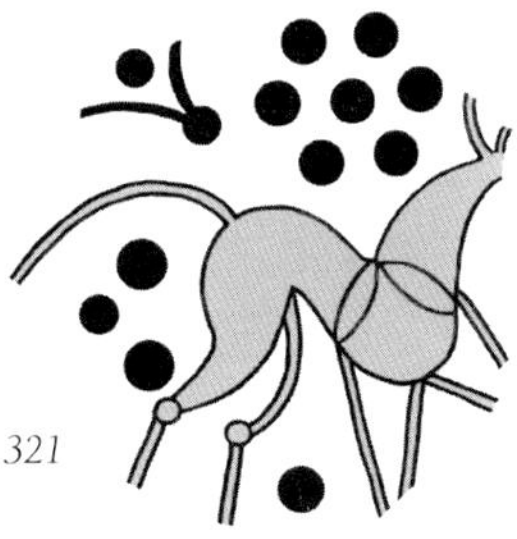

# Type 39 Stork Head Left

**Obliterated obverse.**

**Horse left with stork head, pellet rosette above.**

39a
- pellet above
- pellet below tail

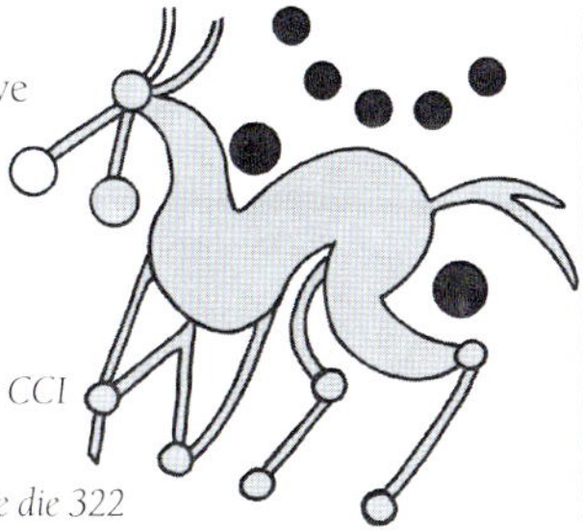

*2 examples in the CCI*
*1 reverse die.*
*Illustrated: reverse die 322*

39b
ABC 1836
BMC 3249-3250
- pellet-triangle below tail

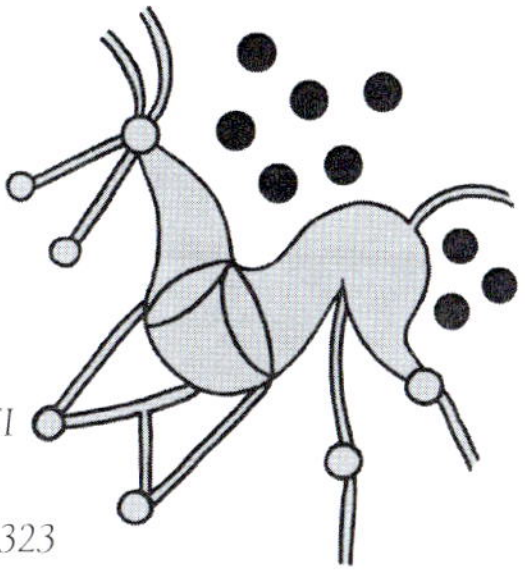

*12 examples in the CCI*
*5 reverse dies.*
*Illustrated: reverse die 323*

39c
- pellet-triangle above tail
- pellet-triangle below head
- pellet below tail

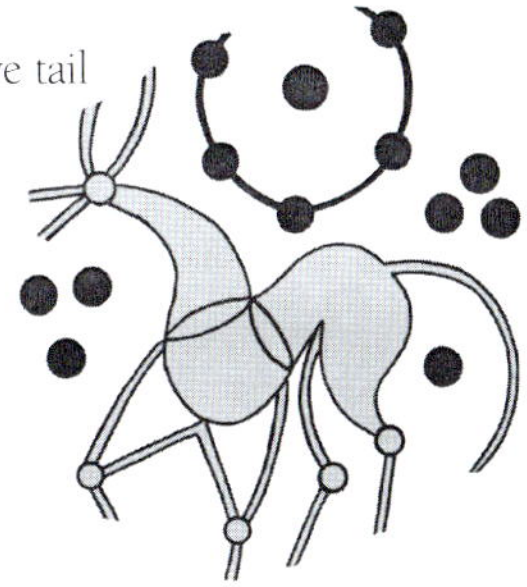

*4 examples in the CCI*
*2 reverse dies.*
*Illustrated: reverse die 328*

# Type 40 Triangle Head

**Obliterated obverse.**

**Horse right with triangular head, pellet rosette above.**

40a
- pellet below head
- pellet below

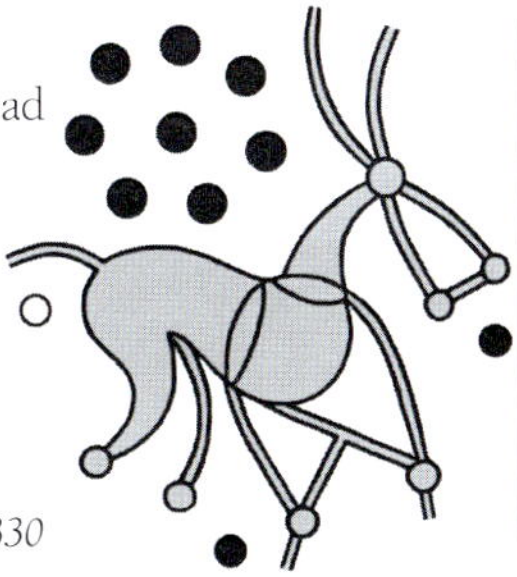

*5 examples in the CCI*
*4 reverse dies.*
*Illustrated: reverse die 330*

40b
- pellet-triangle below tail

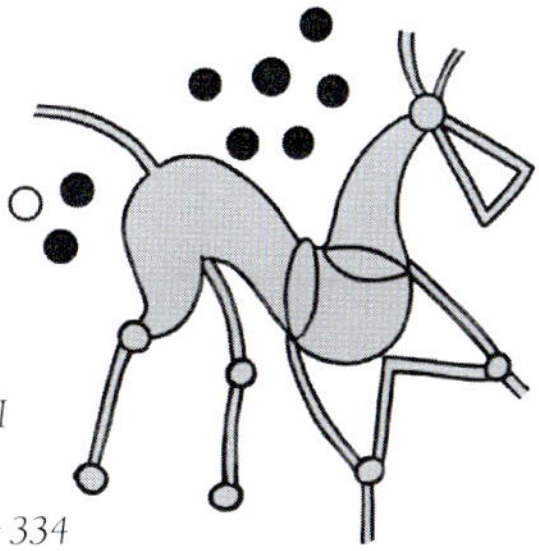

*7 examples in the CCI*
*3 reverse dies*
*Illustrated: reverse die 334*

## Type 41 Mini Kite Left

**Obliterated obverse.**

**Horse left with stork head, 'kite' above.**

41a

VA 889-1
BMC 3246

- 'kite' contains 1 pellet

*6 examples in the CCI.*
*4 reverse dies.*
*Illustrated: reverse die 338*

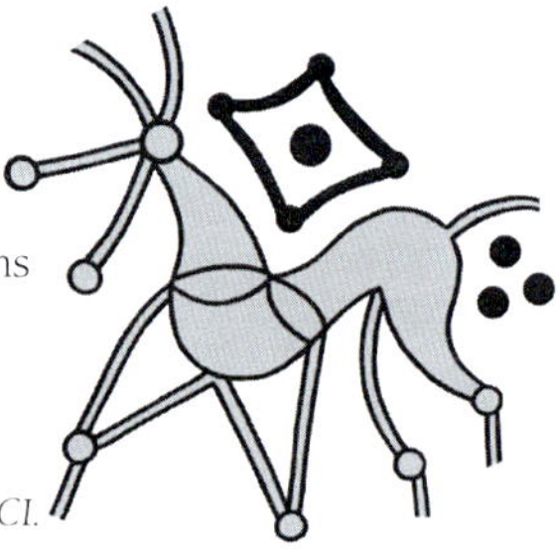

41b

VA 889-3, 889-5
BMC 3247

- 'kite' contains 2 pellets

*3 examples in the CCI.*
*2 reverse dies.*
*Illustrated: reverse die 342*

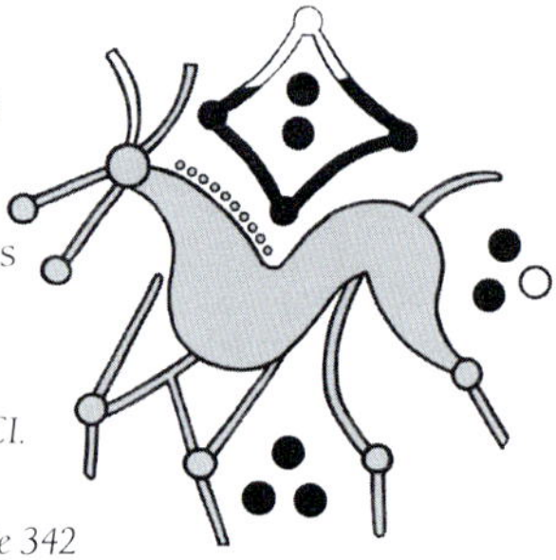

41c
ABC 1839 VA 889-7
BMC 3248

- 'kite' contains 4 pellets

*8 examples in the CCI.*
*3 reverse dies.*
*Illustrated: reverse die 343*

## Type 42 Mini Kite Right

**Obliterated obverse.**

**Horse right with stork head, 'kite' above.**

42

ABC 1842

- 'kite' contains 1 pellet

*4 examples in the Hallaton, Leicestershire hoard (see Leins 2007 BNJ p. 45, illustration 7a)*
*Illustrated: reverse die 346*

# Die Analysis

The series as a whole may be divided into four stages:

**Early period** - unit Types 1-8
**Intermediate period** - unit Types 9-14
**Middle period** - unit Types 15-25, half unit Types 33-36
**Late period** - unit Types 26-32, half unit Types 37-42

## Early period

### Type 1

The series begins with **Type 1a**. The obverse, although based on a Roman prototype, is distinctly British in style. The boar is dominated by an elaborate device of concentric pellet circles, perhaps a solar representation, which takes up nearly half of the design. The pierced boar has four thin but solid legs with distinctive feet, detached ears and a sprawling X with pellet ends above its head. Below the boar is a curious device, commonly referred to a "reversed S", which may represent a rearing snake. Die 6 which is used until extemely worn, is the major obverse die accounting for 17 of the 24 examples of this type and is the only obverse die with multiple reverses.

The handsome horse on the reverse in classical style is probably also derived from a Greek or Roman prototype. It has a forelock and a braided tail (common to all examples of Types 1-5), outstretched legs on a straight exergual line, a mane composed of S's and a large teardrop immediately above the head. In the early stage (die 5) the right rear leg and right foreleg are bifurcated (i.e. shown in outline) but in the later stages both forelegs are bifurcated (see below).

*Type 1a, die 5*

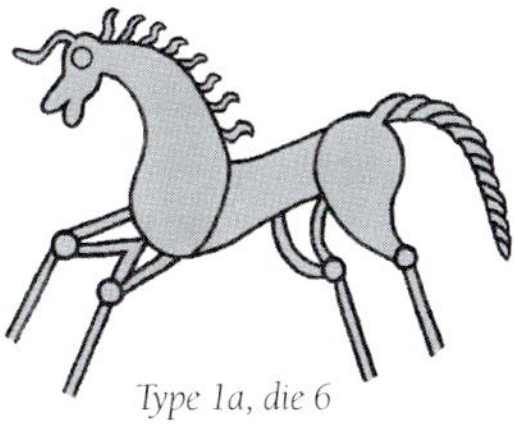

*Type 1a, die 6*

Die 5 is the major reverse die (9 examples) and develops a large flaw below the horse's head (BMC 3194). Die pairing 2/2 (CCI 76.0006, 02.1029) appears to be a contemporary forgery. Reverse die 3 (CCI 98.1917) is re-engraved on die 4 (CCI 00.1198) with a ringed pellet replacing the pellet within the ring above the horse and the ring above the tail moved closer to the pellet ring.

**Type 1b** shares a common obverse with Type 1a but the reverse dies show the horse walking or standing on a curved exergual line with ringed pellets instead of rings around. The teardrop above the horse's head disappears. The horse on die 9 (e.g. CCI 96.2109) has a distinctive lower right rear leg in the shape of a question mark.

Two thirds of Type 1 coins with known findspots are found in north Lincolnshire suggesting that the earliest mint was in the north.

## Type 2

The obverse of **Type 2** is similar in design to Type 1 and retains the ragged cross above the boar's head but the reversed S below the boar is replaced with a normal S with pellet terminals. The left rear leg and right foreleg are now bifurcated. The major die 8 is linked to 6 reverse dies and accounts for 19 of the 23 recorded examples of this type.

The lively horse on the reverse with a long braided tail is similar to Type 1b but the mane has been exaggerated to resemble a line of serpents. All the reverse dies have a straight exergual line running between the horse's feet. Reverse die 15 (e.g. BMC 3201) has a border of S's found later with Type 6.

Like type 1, two thirds of finds for Type 2 occur in north Lincolnshire.

## Type 3

The pierced boar on **Type 3a** has solid forelegs and a bifurcated left rear leg. The ragged cross above the head has been abbreviated to resemble a wishbone and there is nothing below the boar. The horse on the reverse has detached ears and the exaggerated mane of Type 2.

**Type 3b** is noticeably cruder than Type 3a. The wishbone has an additional arm and there are additional pellets within the pellet ring in the solar device. The stocky horse has solid rear legs and a pellet mane and, on one die (die 21), has only one bifurcated foreleg. The two reverse dies 21 and 22 (see below) are used again later in the series.

**Type 3c**, known from a single example, shares a common obverse die (12) with Type 3b and the reverse die (23) is used again later in the series (see below).

## Type 4

Type 4 brings a major change to the the design of the boar which is no longer pierced and has both forelegs bifurcated in a W shape while the left rear leg is shown in a solid curve. The ragged cross is replaced by a large solid X, which later develops a die flaw that extends to the outer ring of the solar device, and the right foreleg of the boar has a distinct "elbow". The solar device is larger than the preceding types with the concentric circles widely spaced and always overlapping the flan. In spite of the change in the obverse design from pierced to unpierced boar, dies 21, 22 and 23, previously paired with obverse die 12, are reused with obverse die 13[4].

**Type 4a**, with a single ringed pellet below the horse, has obverse die 13 paired with reverse dies 24 and 25 and also die 23 previously used with Type 3c. On reverse die 24 the horse stands on a straight exergual line with hatching below and, like Type 3b, has only one bifurcated foreleg.

**Type 4b**, with a pellet ring below the horse and below its head, shares obverse die 13 with Type 4a and has three reverse dies which include two dies (dies 21 and 22) previously used with Type 3b.

**Re-used reverse dies:**

*Type 3b, reverse die 21*
*Re-used with Type 4b*

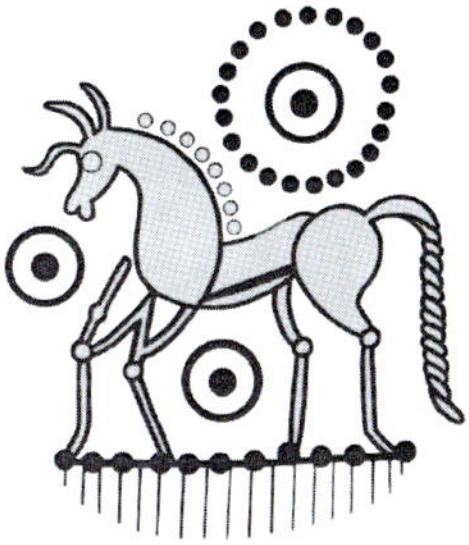

*Type 3b, reverse die 22*
*Re-used with Types 4b & 5d*

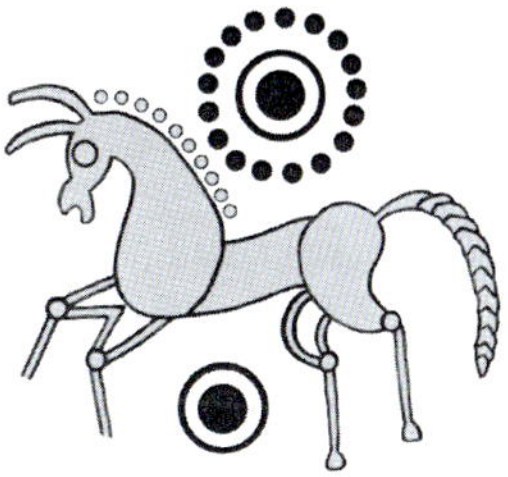

*Type 3c, reverse die 23*
*Re-used with Types 4a & 5e*

## Type 5

On **Type 5a** the "elbow" in the right foreleg of the boar on Type 4 has been modified to a curve and a device of three interlocking S's appears above the tail. The boar has a bushy tail and retains the solid left rear leg from Type 4. The elegant horse on the reverse has a pellet mane (serpent mane on die 29) and continues in the classical style begun with Type 1.

**Type 5b** continues with a modified form of interlocking S's above the tail and there is an S below the boar and the left ear is detached. The right rear leg is bifurcated and the curve in the right foreleg has disappeared.

**Type 5c**, known from a single example in a London sale[5], combines obverse die 17 of Type 5b with reverse die 29 of type 5a.

The boar on **Type 5d** (die 19) is very similar to die 17 but there is a large pellet within the curve of the tail and the ears are not detached. Obverse die 18 has the curved right foreleg of Type 5a. Reverse die 22, which accounts for all five examples of the reverse dies, is recycled from Type 3b.

**Type 5e** shares a common obverse with the preceding type and the reverse die 23, recycled from Type 3c, has now developed a large die flaw above the tail (CCI 95.1355).

**Type 5f** also shares a common obverse with Type 5d. The ringed double pellet within the pellet ring above the horse introduces a new device which is used extensively in succeeding types.

While findspots of Types 1-5 are scattered throughout modern Lincolnshire, over two thirds are found north of Lincoln. The similarity in style suggests a mint in the north.

## Type 6

Type 6 stands apart from Types 1-5. The pierced boar and horse both with solid legs are derived from the earlier types but the style is clearly different. 70% of the few coins with known findspots are concentrated in the south and east of Lincolnshire which may be evidence for a southern mint.

The pierced boar on **Type 6a** appears to have been derived from Type 2 with the ragged cross replaced by a device resembling a large detached ear, and the ringed pellet above the tail replaced by a crescent surmounted by a large pellet, possibly representing the sun and moon, or full and new moon. Like Type 2 the S below the boar has pellet terminals. The horse on the reverse has a long thin curved tail and solid front and rear legs with a border of S's, quite unlike its predecessors (although the border of S's can be seen on some examples of Type 2). The 7 examples in the CCI come from a single obverse die but include 5 reverse dies, a surprisingly large number for what appears to be a relatively small issue.

**Type 6b** is a hybrid of a Type 1a inspired obverse and a Type 6a reverse. The reverse S below the boar has been distorted into a C shape and the rear legs on the horse have been combined. **Type 6c**, known from a single example, has the same obverse but an ugly reverse with a spindly horse with a long tail and detached ears and the sun and moon device has been replaced with a ring within a pellet ring.

## Type 7

While the boar on the obverse of Type 7 continues with the W shaped bifurcated forelegs of Type 5, the reverse is an entirely new design. The horse is belted at the neck and belly, has a large leaf shaped tail with a ringed double pellet above (first seen on Type 5f). The type is a large and complex one with 28 examples including 6 obverse and 11 reverse dies

The obverse boar is the first to be shown with pinhead bristles and has an elbow in the right foreleg (an echo of Type 4). The design is dominated by a double pellet arch above the boar. All three reverse types are linked by the same obverse die (die 25) and are differentiated by the symbol below the horse. On **Type 7a** the horse has an elbow in its left foreleg to mirror the boar, a triplet before and nothing below. On **Type 7b** the elbow disappears, there is no hatching in the tail and there is a ringed pellet below. On **Type 7c** the triplet moves to above the horse's head and there is a ringed double pellet below.

Over 70% of the examples of this type are found in the north of Lincolnshire. Variations between the three types may indicate mint identification marks.

## Type 8

On Type 8 the boar is replaced by a ferocious looking wolf with gaping jaws, presumably based on the tribal emblem of the neighbouring tribe of the Iceni. While the Icenian wolf may have been the inspiration, the style is distinctly Corieltavian with bifurcated fore and rear legs.

There are two styles of horse, one with a fern tail, in anticipation of the change that takes place from Type 11, and the other with a leaf tail which provides a link to Type 7 and which is found on some Icenian silver[6]. The average weight of 1.34g places it early in the series.

The use of the wolf on this rare type suggests it may have been issued to commemorate some specific event, perhaps a treaty with, or victory over, the Iceni. Of the 5 examples with known findspots only 1 is found north of Horncastle in central Lincolnshire.

## Intermediate period

The Intermediate Period marks the transition between the classical style of the Early Period and the prolific issues of the Middle and Late Periods. The variety of types is large but the number of surviving examples is small (only 51 examples covering 19 different types). There are two styles of boar, one where the bifurcated left legs and solid right legs are shown alternately, and one where the bifurcated left legs are centrally placed between the solid right legs. The horse always has a fern tail, a sure method of identifying coins in this class.

### Type 9

Type 9 introduces an entirely new boar and horse. The long legged boar has solid right legs shown alternately to the bifurcated left legs and has long pinhead bristles. The youthful looking horse now has a long fern tail and a mane of dashes. A feature of the type is the increasing length of the forelegs of the horse and the extensive use of ringed double and triple pellets. Type 9 is an extremely rare type with only 12 examples in the CCI and marks the transition to Type 10. None of the sub-types of Type 9 is die linked to each other.

The sole example of **Type 9a** has a line running from the boar's head to a ringed triple pellet below. There is a ringed triple pellet above the boar and within the pellet ring above the horse which has a spiral above its tail. **Type 9b** is a variation of 9a but the ringed triple pellet above the boar is replaced by a pellet within a pellet ring and there are scattered wedges in the field. The spiral above the horse's tail is now below the horse's head.

The line to the ringed triple pellet below the boar's head is broken on **Type 9c** which has a horse of different style with a pinhead mane and a belt around its narrow waist with scattered wedges, found on Type 9b, now below the horse's tail.

The boar on the sole example of **Type 9d** is dominated by a large ringed double pellet within a pellet ring above, which takes up over half the flan, and the ringed triple pellet is now above the boar's head and below the horse.

On **Type 9e** the ringed pellet within pellet ring appears below the boar instead of above, possibly a striking error caused by initially cutting the boar too high in the die, and there is a vestige of the line running below the boar's head. The forelegs of the boar revert to the W shape.

The boar with muddled legs on **Type 9f** is a crude representation of type 9b with the reverse based on Type 9e.

### Type 10

Type 10 brings another major change in the style of the boar: The two inner legs (left rear and left fore) are bifurcated while the two outer legs are solid. This design continues until Type 14. Obverse die variations for Types 11-14 are subtle, often depending on the direction of the bristles on the boar or the shape of its rear leg.

The boar on **Type 10a**, with its dense pincushion bristles and ringed double pellets below and below its head, and the horse with its long fern tail, continues the style of Type 9. **Type 10b** is similar except for the symbols above the boar and below the horse.

## Type 11

There is a marked change in style from the previous types. The boar is deep chested with a broad snout, straight bristles and spiral below its tail and the pellet ring above contains a ringed double pellet. The horse has a short fern tail (shorter than Types 9 and 10) and exaggerated forelegs.

Successive die links determine the order of Types 11a-11b-12a-12b-13a-13b.

The horse on **Type 11a** has over-long forelegs and a pinhead mane and is die linked to **Type 11b** which has a similar horse and even longer overlapping fore and rear legs. Type 11 is rare with only 6 examples known.

## Type 12

The boar on **Type 12a** has clawed feet while the distinctive horse has a diagonal bar running from the ear through the mane. The forelegs are even further extended with a divided right foreleg and a single left foreleg. The type is die linked to Type 11a and 11b.

**Type 12b** is identical to Type 12a except for the ringed pellet below the horse.

## Type 13

**Type 13a** is die-linked to Type 12a. The major obverse die (die 43) has a faint line running from the boar's foreleg to its snout. The horse on the reverse now has a long tail stranded on one side with two ringed double pellets within a pellet ring above. Three examples of the type have substantially reduced weights: CCI 95.2651 (0.72g), 96.3095 (0.72g) and 01.1703 (0.77g) with a full design struck on a thinner flan.

The obverse of **Type 13b** is die linked to Type 13a and the reverse is an elaborate version of the same coin. The boar has one solid right foreleg and the horse one solid left foreleg.

## Type 14

There are only five examples of Type 14 in the CCI. **Type 14a** has a handsome boar with forward facing bristles and a robust fern tailed horse with a ringed concave triangle below. **Type 14b** is an inferior version of the same coin but with a ringed double pellet below the horse's head.

The horse on **Type 14c** has a single left foreleg inherited from Type 13b with a distinctive Mercedes symbol below.

# Middle period

Just over 50% of the total production of the boar/horse series takes place during the Middle

Period[7] which commences with a boar with two W shaped bifurcated forelegs and two solid rear legs and a horse with a simple straight tail. This brief interlude is soon followed by the final stage where the forelegs of the boar are combined into a single Y shape.

## Type 15

Type 15 is very rare with only 4 examples in the CCI. For the first time in the series the horse faces right instead of left and has a long thin tail. This may indicate a different mint but only one find spot from Snettisham in Norfolk is known.

**Type 15a** has a new symbol above the boar: double pellets within a pellet ring which reappears much later in the series with Type 22. There are wheels before and behind the boar and the wheel motif is repeated above the horse. This rare device appears only once more in the series (although it reappears later on half units). The horse has pellet triangles above its head and tail, the first introduction of a symbol which is used extensively in the rest of the series. On **Type 15b**, known from a single specimen found at Snettisham, the triple pellets appear above the boar's head and tail with a spiral below and there is a wheel above the horse.

## Type 16

Type 16 is a prolific issue with 46 examples of Type 16a and 33 examples of Type 16b in the CCI and the condition of the surviving coins, many worn almost to obliteration, indicates a long period of circulation.

**Type 16a** has 3 major obverse dies, one with a boar with crossed-over forelegs (die 51) linked to 4 reverse dies, one with a boar with long curved ears and feet with long clawlike toes standing on an exergual line (die 52) linked to 5 reverse dies of Type 16a and 2 reverse dies of Type 16b, and one with an overlarge pellet ring above the boar (die 50). In all cases with this type the plump horse has a pellet mane but is without a ringed pellet above its tail. Die 52 is used until almost complete obliteration. Reverse die 88 is linked to obverse die 53 from Type 16b.

**Type 16b** has only 2 obverse dies (1 from Type 10a) and all the examples in the CCI show evidence of considerable wear. The horse, similar in style to Type 16a, has lost its pellet mane but has gained a ringed pellet above its tail.

Three half units[8], all with obliterated obverses, are struck on Type 16b reverse dies; two with reverse die 90 (0.58 gm and 0.39 gm) and one with reverse die 91 (BMC 3210, 0.58g), perhaps early experimental issues.

**Type 16c**, known from only 2 examples, has a long legged boar with a spiral under its tail, first used in the Intermediate Period. The skinny horse on Type 16d has bands around its neck and belly and a pellet below its tail.

**Type 16e**, known from a single example, is a curious coin clearly linked to the previous type. The boar has the clawed feet seen in Types 12 and 16a and W shaped forelegs with a pronounced Y in the rightmost foreleg which appears to be a transition to the final stage of Type 18.

## Type 17

The pierced boar with W shaped forelegs and combined solid rear legs makes a brief reappearance possibly due to the die engraver copying an old die. The kneeling horse appears for the first time on **Type 17a** which shares the same obverse die with **Type 17b**, the latter known from one poor quality example.

## Types 18-19

Type 18 signals the last major change in the style of the boar with the W shaped forelegs now combined into a single Y shape, a style that remains unchanged for the rest of the series. This major change is accompanied by a sudden increase in weight with three examples of Type 18a over 1.30g.[9] However, this increase was short lived and the average weight of later coins soon drops back to about 1.25g.

The boar on **Type 18a** has an elaborate curly tail, prominent feet and widely spaced bristles and the kneeling horse continues the style from Type 17. The boar on the sole example of **Type 18b** has a star below its head, the only use of this symbol in the series, and the kneeling horse has a pellet triangle below its head, the forerunner of Type 19.

The kneeling horse on Type 19 has a distinctive ladder mane. There is only one example of **Type 19a** which is die-linked to Type 18b. The horse has a wheel above and concave triangle below its head which is replaced by a pellet triangle on **Type 19b**.

## Type 20

Only two examples of this coin are known, both from different dies, one from Glinton in Cambridgeshire and the other from Sleaford.The ladder bristles on the boar are apparently derived from the ladder mane of the horse on Type 19 but the style of the coin with the double ring below the boar and above the horse is unique in the series.

## Type 21

Type 21 has a deep chested boar with Y shaped forelegs and ringed pellets above and below. The tail of the boar starts to creep upwards until it becomes finally detached on Type 22.

The single rear leg of the boar and the kneeling horse on **Type 21a** continues the style of types 17-20. On **Type 21b** the boar acquires a second rear leg which continues for the rest of the series.The horse is in now in a standing position.

On **Type 21c** the horse has a torc under its tufted tail and extended forelegs and on **Type 21d** the boar with abnormally long bristles on the obverse die has three different reverse dies showing a diminutive horse also with a tufted tail.

## Type 22

Type 22 introduces another major change with the horse now facing right which continues until the nearly the end of the series. This type is one of the largest in the series with 87 examples in the CCI from 26 obverse and 26 reverse dies.

On **Type 22a** the design of the handsome compact boar on die 70 soon deteriorates on dies 71-78 to a poorly engraved elongated version extending to either side of the flan.Most examples are well worn.

The boar and horse on **Type 22b** are surmounted by double pellets within a pellet ring, seldom completely visible.The style of the boar is elongated and thin with deep Y shaped forelegs and long ears.Two of the reverse dies (dies 126 and 130) develop die flaws, the former extending across the entire coin. **Type 22c** is a simplified and coarser version of Type 22b: the detached tail on the elongated boar has moved to above the rump and the horse has a long neck with the head invariably off the flan.

35 (68%) of Type 22 coins with known findspots are found in north Lincolnshire.

## Type 23

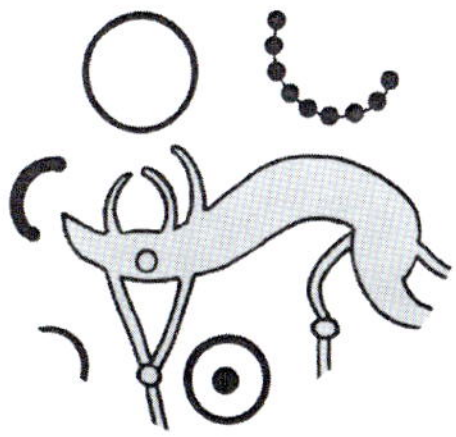

*Type 23, die 96*

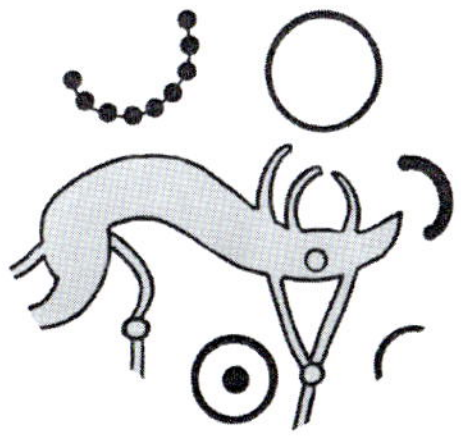

*Reverse image*

At first sight this coin, known from a single example (CCI 93.0808), appears to be a brockage of Type 22c but reversal of the image matches no known die. The boar, with a ring above its head and a ringed pellet below, and the horse, with a pellet triangle below its tail, are otherwise unknown, and the left facing boar must be a deliberate strike.

## Type 24

Type 24 is by far the largest type in the series with 154 examples in the CCI and marks the final stage of the evolution of the boar which now has a tightly curled shrimp-like body, long wide spaced bristles, exaggerated Y forelegs and an upturned snout. In many ways this design is the most beautiful in the series.

There is a great similarity in all the sub-types which are separately identified by the symbols around the boar and horse. **Type 24a** has rings around the boar and below the horse. **Type 24b**, die flawed and known only from two worn examples, has a ring below the boar and a ringed pellet below the horse, and **Type 24c** has rings above and below the boar and horse and a pellet below their respective tails.

**Type 24d** with pellets below the horse and boar's tail and a ring below the boar is a large group with 38 examples in the CCI. The dies, almost without exception, are well worn and there is a die flaw on reverse die 150.

**Type 24e** with pellets below the boar and horse's tail is the largest group and at some stage during the production of this type a decision must have been made to cease engraving new obverse dies. Of the 99 examples of this type in the CCI, 41 are either extremely worn beyond the point of identification or completely obliterated, while examples that can be identified are invariably well worn. This indicates massive output over a short period of time with perhaps the obverse dies abandoned to speed output. Many of the dies are too large for the flan, with the head of the boar and horse seldom visible. There are 60 coins of this type with known findspots of which 45 were found in north Lincolnshire.

There is a brockage of obverse die 112 (CCI 03.1194) as well as a unit (reverse die 176) struck on a half unit flan (CCI 02.1125).

**Type 24f** has no symbols around the boar or horse and includes a curiosity, a die flawed 24f reverse (die 187) with an obverse die from Type 18a (die 59); presumably an old die from the beginning of the Middle Period used by the engraver in error (CCI 95.1354).

66 (72%) of the 92 known findspots for Type 24 occur in north Lincolnshire including 23 from South Ferriby, 15 from Caistor and 8 from Kirmington.

### Type 25

**Type 25a** is known from only two examples, one from the South Ferriby hoard (Allen 306), and has a pellet triangle above the boar's head and below the horse. Type 25b, also known from a single worn example from the South Ferriby hoard (Allen 307), has the same obverse as Type 25a but a ringed pellet below the horse.

**Type 25c**, known from four examples, two from the South Ferriby hoard (Allen 305 & 308), has a bold ringed pellet above the horse. All the obverse dies are well worn or obliterated.

## Late period

All coins from the Late Period have obliterated obverses, some with faint traces of the boar and many with completely blank flans. The forelegs of the horse become an important feature of the design and the average weight of the coins drops rapidly from above 1.2g to below 1g. The head of the horse defines the classification of the coins.

### Type 26

On Type 26 the horse faces right and has a natural head, often difficult to identify because it is generally off the flan. It is banded at the neck and belly and has elongated forelegs. Obverse dies may have faint markings or are completely smooth.

**Type 26a** has no symbols around the horse. The 12 examples in the CCI come from 5 different dies. **Type 26b** has a detached right foreleg (a common feature of the type) and a pellet under the tail. **Type 26c** is known from a single example and has a pellet below the horse and below the tail.

All 10 examples of **Type 26d**, with the pellet triangle below the tail, are extremely worn; 6 come from the South Ferriby hoard. The horse on **Type 26e**, with the pellet triangle below, has a detached right foreleg.

All the 6 examples of **Type 26f** with the pellet triangle before the head come from the same die which develops a large die-flaw along the right foreleg.

The 8 examples of **Type 26g**, with pellet triangles below and below the head, also come from the same die and the horse has the familiar detached foreleg. Finally **Type 26h** has a profusion of pellet triangles, below the head, below the tail and below.

Examples of Type 26 are well spread with 18 examples found in north Lincolnshire, 10 in the east, 1 in the south, 3 in Cambridgeshire, I in Norfolk and 2 in Northamptonshire.

## Type 27

On Type 27 the horse faces left and has a natural head, again usually off the flan. The average weight of this type drops abruptly from 1.21g to 1.04g. The horse is banded at the neck and belly and is of a more delicate style than Type 26 with shorter forelegs but longer ears and rear legs.

There is only one example of **Type 27a** which has a pellet below the horse and below its tail. There are 14 examples from 4 dies of **Type 27b** with the pellet triangle below the horse and a distinctive ringed pellet above the tail. **Type 27c** has a pellet triangle below the tail and below. Small flans mean that these symbols are seldom completely visible.

In contrast to Type 26, 7 of the 9 examples of Type 27 come from the south, including 4 found in Cambridgeshire. This distribution, combined with the stylistic differences and lower weight may indicate two mints at work, one in the north and one in the south.

## Type 28

On type 28 the horse has a stork head perhaps influenced by the triangular head of the South Ferriby staters (ABC 1743-1752) and faces right. There is a noticeable increase in weight and the change in style is accompanied by a graceful horse with long legs with a bold pellet ring above. Obverse dies are now worn completely smooth. The stork headed type continues for the rest of the series.

**Type 28a** with a pellet below the tail is the largest sub-type with 62 examples from 18 dies. Die 220 develops a progressive flaw; first a line between the front legs of the horse followed by a flaw on the rump[10]. There is also an example struck on a half-unit die (CCI 97.1503). There are only two examples of **Type 28b** with the pellet triangle below the tail (visible only on CCI 00.0195) and only one of **Type 28c** which has a pellet cross below the horse, unique in the series.

Type 28 findspots are well scattered with 18 found in north Lincolnshire, 11 in east Lincolnshire, 2 in south Lincolnshire, 1 in Norfolk, 2 in Cambridgeshire, I in Nottinghamshire, I in Staffordshire and I in Essex.

### Type 29

**Type 29** is a rare type with a stork headed horse facing left. There are only two examples in the CCI. The horse appears to have a pellet triangle below the tail (CCI 96.2156).

### Types 30-32

The three final types are all directly influenced by the accompanying staters, ABC 1743-1761, the only time in the series where there is a direct connection between the gold and silver coinage. Note, however, that the portrayal of the horse remains the same and does not adopt the abstract style of the gold coinage.

On **Type 30** the horse faces left and has the triangular head of the South Ferriby staters, ABC 1743-52. Below the horse is an elaborate cross with pellets in each angle, the only use of this symbol in the series.

On **Type 31** the horse is surmounted by a "domino" derived from ABC 1758. The four examples in the CCI come from three different dies and all show excessive wear.

On **Type 32** the long necked horse (the head is never visible) faces left and is surmounted by a "kite" derived from ABC 1761. Like Type 31 all surviving examples are extremely worn. On **Type 32a** the kite encloses 1 pellet and on **Type 32b** 4 pellets. The latter type also has a pellet triangle below the tail.

Until the discovery of the Hallaton hoard[11] only 6 examples of this type were known. The hoard uncovered a further 72 examples found together within large numbers of inscribed Corieltavian coins, confirmation that this type comes right at the end of the uninscribed series.

## Half Units

The introduction of half units appears to have taken place during the Middle Period during the production of unit Type 24. Prior to this there had been random test strikings (perhaps accidental) with Types 10a and 15a and later on with 24e and 30a. The shrimp-like style of the boar on Type 33, the first half-unit type, closely matches the style of unit Type 24. This is supported by an analysis of the South Ferriby hoard (see appendix) which contained 50 uninscribed units and 14 half units. The earliest unit was Type 24d and the earliest half unit was Type 33a.

Over 70% of the 171 known findspots for half units are in the north of Lincolnshire.

## Middle period

### Type 33

**Type 33a** has a single obverse die (die 130), a masterpiece of Iron Age die engraving. The right facing boar is surrounded by ringed pellets and "bear paws" with a curious symbol resembling a long tailed rearing serpent before. There are 4 reverse dies showing a solid looking horse with a wheel above and a star below. Of the 6 examples with findspots, 5 come from north Lincolnshire. All surviving examples are well worn.

The obverse of Type 33a is die linked to **Type 33b** which has a horse with a wheel above and a ring below. On **Type 33c** the obverse is partly obliterated (possibly die 130) and the horse has a wheel above and a pellet under its tail. The 4 examples of **Type 33d** all come from Caistor (3 from the same hoard) and appear to be an unfinished trial striking for die 130 and confirm Caistor as a probable mint site.

### Type 34

The boar on **Type 34a** faces in the opposite direction, although obviously based on Type 33a, and has a wheel instead of a pellet ring above. All surviving examples are extremely worn, the obverse dies to the point of obliteration. The lively horse on the reverse (die 255) has a distinctive hooked right rear foot.

The boar on **Type 34b**, known only from two badly worn examples, is a poor copy of Type 34a and the clumsy horse has a single foreleg. All 3 examples of **Type 34c** have extremely worn obverse dies derived from Type 34a, while the reverse has a horse with a deep chest and raised rump.

### Type 35

5 of the 7 examples of Type 35 with known findspots come from Caistor and the other two from Manton and Dragonby, all in the north of Lincolnshire. The simplified boar and horse, without bristles or mane, are executed in bold thick lines.

**Type 35a** has a four spoked wheel above the boar and the horse and a star below the horse. The shrimp-like boar on **Type 35b** has a detached double tail and the horse lacks the star.

### Type 36

The single example of **Type 36a** is badly chipped with most details missing but the boar is evidently based on Type 33a with a wheel above and below the boar's snout. **Type 36b** has a distinctive boar with very long bristles and the horse has a pellet below the tail.

## Late period

### Type 37

The horse on uniface Type 37 faces left and has a natural head and is the corresponding half unit to Type 27. The obverse dies are very worn or completely obliterated and no new obverse dies are cut and the old dies are used until smooth.

The horse on **Type 37a** has a long neck with a mane of dashes and a pellet under the tail. On 6 of the 8 dies part of the left foreleg is completely detached from the body. The type is the most common half unit with 33 examples in the CCI. On **Type 37b** the foreleg is similarly detached while the dashed mane is linked to the pellet ring above the horse and the pellet below the tail is replaced by a pellet triangle.

26 (79%) of the 33 examples of Types 35a and 35b come from north Lincolnshire.

**Type 37c** is known from only three examples and has an inverted L between the forelegs. The horses on **Types 37d** and **37e** both have pellets between widely splayed forelegs. Of the 8 examples of Types 37c-37d, 2 come from Ancaster and 4 from Thistleton in Rutland, all in the south.

## Type 38

The horse on Type 38 faces right and has a stork head, and is the corresponding half unit for unit Type 28. Altogether there are 82 examples in this class from 38 dies embracing 11 different types which are determined by the arrangement of symbols around the horse.

**Type 38a**, known from a single example from Ancaster, has no ornaments around the horse. **Type 38b** with a pellet under the tail is a relatively common type (20 examples). Obverse die 289 has faint traces of the left facing boar of Type 32. **Type 38c** has a large ringed pellet below the horse. **Type 38d** with the pellet triangle below the horse has 3 different dies from only 5 examples, all from the Kirmington/South Ferriby area and rare **Type 38e** has a ringed pellet within the pellet ring above the horse.

**Type 38f**, with a pellet triangle below the tail, is also relatively common (19 examples) and **Type 38g** has a pellet above and below the jaws of the stork head. **Type 38h**, with pellet triangles below the tail and below, is a common type with 13 different dies from 25 examples.

The sole example of **Type 38i** has a pellet triangle above the horse's neck and the equally rare **Type 38j** has the corner of a box, perhaps a kite, above the tail.

44 (71%) of the 62 examples of Type 38 were found in north Lincolnshire, 17 at Caistor.

## Type 39

The stork headed horse on Type 39 faces left and is the half unit for unit Type 29. One of the two examples of **Type 39a**, with a stranded tail and a pellet below, comes from South Ferriby.

Three examples of **Type 39b** (2 of die 323 and 1 of die 326) are engraved with a reversed S on an otherwise blank flan. The horse has a pellet triangle below the tail.

**Type 39c** has a pellet triangle below the head and above the tail.

## Type 40

The horse on Type 40 faces right and has a triangular head, derived from the South Ferriby stater and is related to the left facing horse in unit Type 30. There are only 5 examples of **Type 40a** with pellets below the horse and below the horse's muzzle but they come from 4 different dies, 3 in the CCI and one example sold by a dealer in 2010. **Type 40b** has a pellet triangle under the tail.

Some examples omit the closing bar to the head and may appear stork headed.

## Type 41

Type 41 with the "kite" above the horse is derived from the accompanying stater ABC 1761 and is the half unit for unit Type 32. There are three types with the horse facing left: **Type 41a** with a kite containing one pellet, **Type 41b** with two and **Type 41c** with four.
The Hallaton hoard[12] produced 9 examples of this type.

## Type 42

**Type 42** was unknown until the discovery of 4 examples in the Hallaton hoard. The horse faces right and the kite contains a single pellet.

**14.** *The Rothwell Boar bronze figurine, c.1st century BC/AD, 55mm long, 35mm high, was found by a metal detectorist in 1990 at Rothwell Top, near Caistor, Lincs., only 18 miles from where the famous boar-faced Witham Shield was dredged from the river Witham, near Lincoln, in 1826.* Ex Chris Rudd List 92, *March 2007, now in The Collection, Lincoln Museum.*

# Die chains

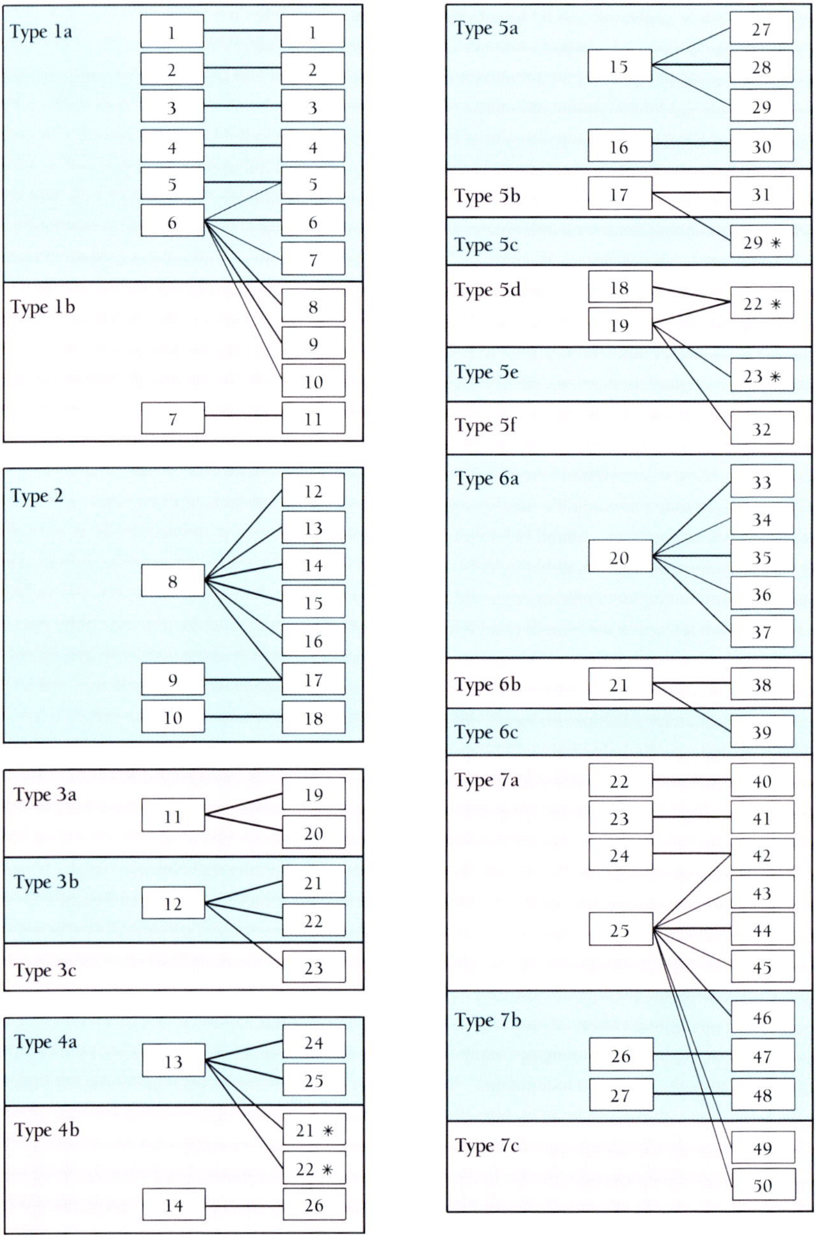


∗ re -used dies

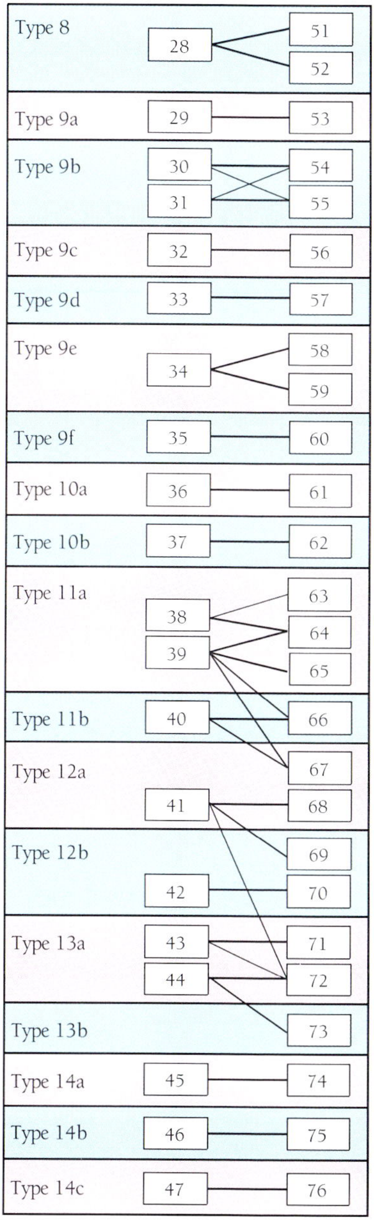
Type 8
28
51
52
Type 9a
29
53
Type 9b
30
31
54
55
Type 9c
32
56
Type 9d
33
57
Type 9e
34
58
59
Type 9f
35
60
Type 10a
36
61
Type 10b
37
62
Type 11a
38
39
63
64
65
Type 11b
40
66
Type 12a
67
41
68
Type 12b
69
42
70
Type 13a
43
71
44
72
Type 13b
73
Type 14a
45
74
Type 14b
46
75
Type 14c
47
76

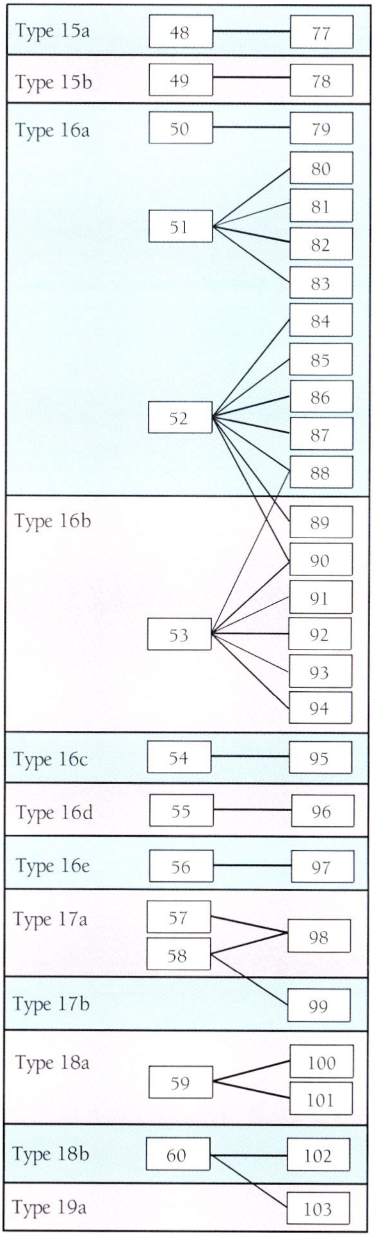
Type 15a
48
77
Type 15b
49
78
Type 16a
50
79
80
81
51
82
83
84
85
86
52
87
88
Type 16b
89
90
91
53
92
93
94
Type 16c
54
95
Type 16d
55
96
Type 16e
56
97
Type 17a
57
58
98
Type 17b
99
Type 18a
100
59
101
Type 18b
60
102
Type 19a
103

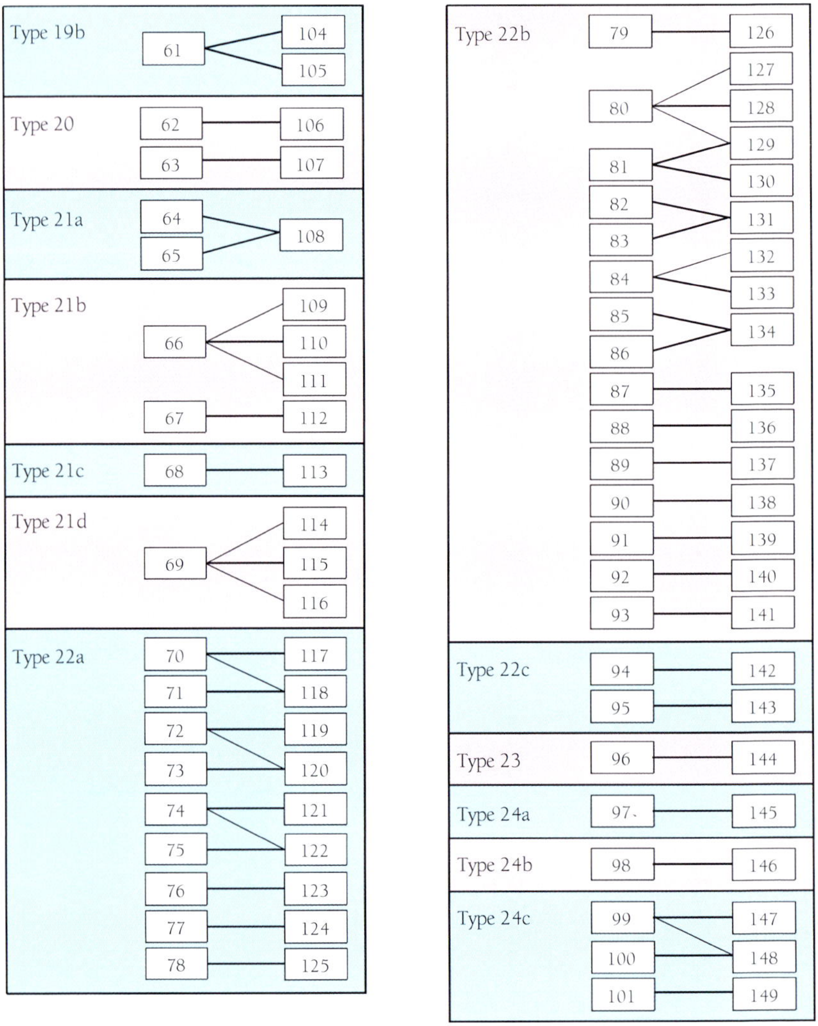
Type 19b
61
104
105
Type 20
62
106
63
107
Type 21a
64
65
108
Type 21b
66
109
110
111
67
112
Type 21c
68
113
Type 21d
69
114
115
116
Type 22a
70
117
71
118
72
119
73
120
74
121
75
122
76
123
77
124
78
125
Type 22b
79
126
127
80
128
129
81
130
82
131
83
132
84
133
85
134
86
87
135
88
136
89
137
90
138
91
139
92
140
93
141
Type 22c
94
142
95
143
Type 23
96
144
Type 24a
97
145
Type 24b
98
146
Type 24c
99
147
100
148
101
149

# DIE CHAIN - UNITS

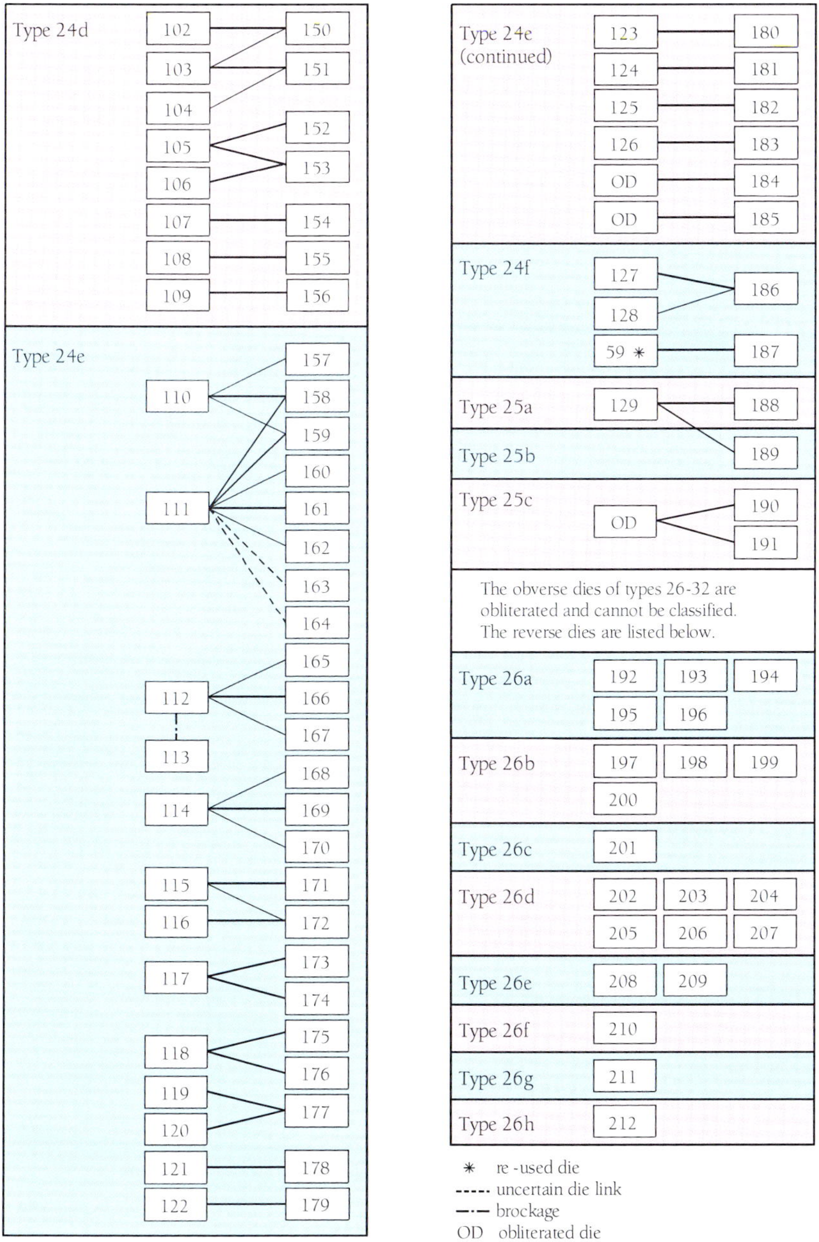


* re -used die
----- uncertain die link
—·— brockage
OD obliterated die

| Type | Dies | | |
|---|---|---|---|
| Type 27a | 213 | | |
| Type 27b | 214 | 215 | 216 |
| | 217 | | |
| Type 27c | 218 | 219 | |
| Type 28a | 220 | 221 | 222 |
| | 223 | 224 | 225 |
| | 226 | 227 | 228 |
| | 229 | 230 | 231 |
| | 232 | 233 | 234 |
| | 235 | 236 | 237 |
| Type 28b | 238 | | |
| Type 28c | 239 | | |
| Type 29 | 240 | 241 | |
| Type 30 | 242 | | |
| Type 31 | 243 | 244 | 245 |
| Type 32a | 246 | | |
| Type 32b | 247 | | |

**15.** *The spoked wheel may represent the sun. Rich Type 35a.*

**Half Units**

| Type | Obverse die | Reverse die |
|---|---|---|
| Type 33a | 130 | 248 |
| | 130 | 249 |
| | 130 | 250 |
| | 130 | 251 |
| Type 33b | 130 | 252 |
| Type 33c | 130 (uncertain die link) | 253 |
| Type 33d | 131 | 254 |
| Type 34a | 132 | 255 |
| | 132 | 256 |
| | 132 | 257 |
| Type 34b | 133 | 258 |
| | 134 | 258 |
| Type 34c | 135 | 259 |
| Type 35a | 136 | 260 |
| Type 35b | 137 | 261 |
| | 138 | 262 |
| Type 36a | 139 | 263 |
| Type 36b | 140 | 264 |

The obverse dies of types 37-42 are obliterated and cannot be classified. The reverse dies are listed below.

| Type | Reverse dies | | |
|---|---|---|---|
| Type 37a | 265 | 266 | 267 |
| | 268 | 269 | 270 |
| | 271 | 272 | |
| Type 37b | 273 | 274 | 275 |
| | 276 | | |

----- uncertain die link

| | |
|---|---|
| Type 37c | 277, 278 |
| Type 37d | 279, 280, 281, 282 |
| Type 37e | 283, 284 |
| Type 38a | 285 |
| Type 38b | 286, 287, 288, 289, 290, 291, 292 |
| Type 38c | 293 |
| Type 38d | 294, 295, 296 |
| Type 38e | 297 |
| Type 38f | 298, 299, 300, 301, 302, 303, 304 |
| Type 38g | 305, 306 |
| Type 38h | 307, 308, 309, 310, 311, 312, 313, 314, 315, 316, 317, 318, 319 |
| Type 38i | 320 |
| Type 38j | 321 |
| Type 39a | 322 |
| Type 39b | 323, 324, 325, 326, 327 |
| Type 39c | 328, 329 |

| | |
|---|---|
| Type 40a | 330, 331, 332, 333 |
| Type 40b | 334, 335, 336 |
| Type 41a | 337, 338, 339, 340 |
| Type 41b | 341, 342 |
| Type 41c | 343, 344, 345 |
| Type 42 | 346 |

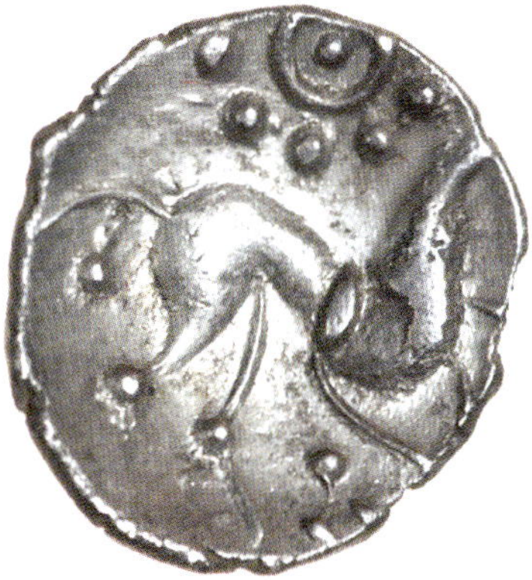

**16.** *Rich Type 38e.*

**17.** *Rich Type 41c.*

# Weight Analysis

| UNITS | | |
|---|---|---|
| Type | Average weight (gms) | No. of coins in sample * |
| 1 | 1.41 | 15 |
| 2 | 1.42 | 10 |
| 3 | 1.38 | 6 |
| 4 | 1.41 | 8 |
| 5 | 1.41 | 11 |
| 6 | 1.37 | 6 |
| 7 | 1.34 | 16 |
| 8 | 1.34 | 6 |
| 9 | 1.33 | 7 |
| 10 | 1.35 | 2 |
| 11 | 1.24 | 4 |
| 12 | 1.39 | 1 |
| 13 | 1.34 | 5 |
| 14 | 1.26 | 3 |
| 15 | 1.36 | 3 |
| 16 | 1.31 | 40 |
| 17 | 1.28 | 2 |
| 18 | 1.33 | 5 |
| 19 | 1.23 | 3 |
| 20 | 1.19 | 1 |
| 21 | 1.27 | 9 |
| 22 | 1.27 | 40 |
| 23 | 1.35 | 1 |
| 24 | 1.24 | 59 |
| 25 | 1.21 | 6 |
| 26 | 1.21 | 22 |
| 27 | 1.04 | 8 |
| 28 | 1.09 | 49 |
| 29 | | 0 |
| 30 | 0.92 | 2 |
| 31 | 0.87 | 3 |
| 32 | 0.94 | 3 |

* chipped or excessively worn coins excluded from the sample

| HALF UNITS | | |
|---|---|---|
| Type | Average weight (gms) | No. of coins in sample * |
| 33 | 0.56 | 12 |
| 34 | 0.51 | 16 |
| 35 | 0.53 | 10 |
| 36 | 0.49 | 3 |
| 37 | 0.49 | 28 |
| 38 | 0.45 | 57 |
| 39 | 0.43 | 13 |
| 40 | 0.45 | 5 |
| 41 | 0.43 | 11 |
| 42 | | 0 |

**18.** *Rich Type 16b, W-Forelegs Proto Boar, with three ringed-pellets (solar symbols?) around the horse.*

| **Average Weight** | Units | Half Units | |
|---|---|---|---|
| Early Period (1-8) | 1.39g | | |
| Intermediate Period (9-14) | 1.31g | | |
| Middle Period (15-25) | 1.27g | (33-36) | 0.53g |
| Late Period (26-32) | 1.10g | (37-42) | 0.46g |

# Distribution

1,163 units and 551 half units are recorded in the CCI. Of these 532 units and 246 half units have recorded find spots. Analysis of these findspots shows that 84% of the units and 88% of the half units were found within the modern boundary of Lincolnshire, a remarkably concentrated distribution pattern for a long lived series.

## Distribution of Units

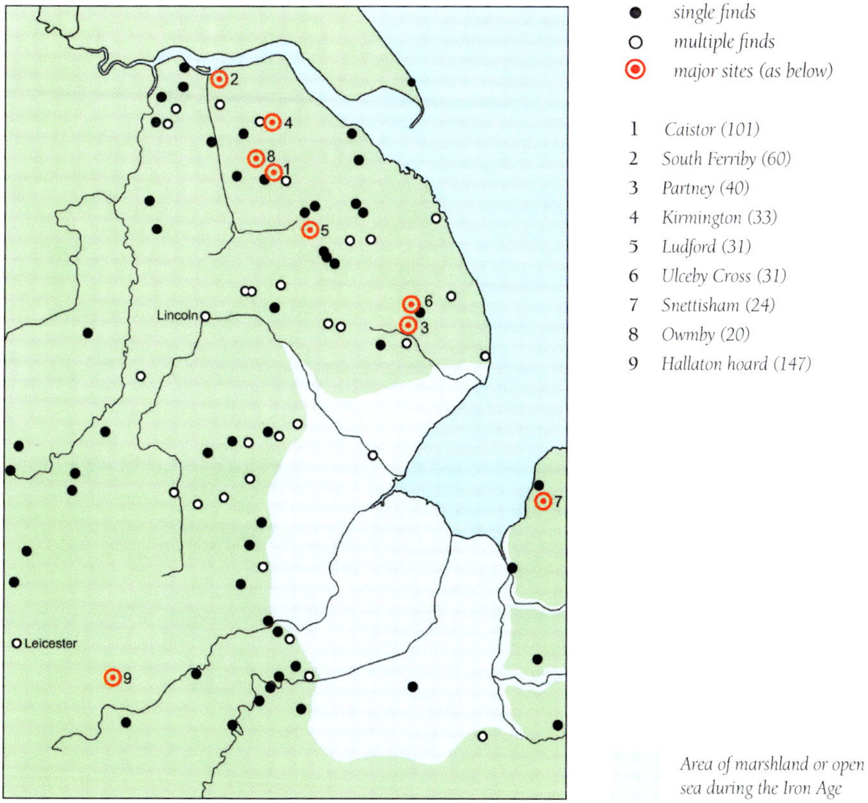


**19.** *Distribution of silver units. Excludes finds outside the boundary of the map, i.e.: Berkshire (1), Cambridgeshire (1), Cheshire (1), Essex (1), Herfordshire (1), Norfolk (4), Northamptonshire (3), Oxfordshire (1), Staffordshire (1), Suffolk (2), Warwickshire (2), Yorkshire (4).*

Unit finds are widely scattered from the Humber river in the north to Cambridgeshire in the south and to Nottinghamshire and Leicestershire in the west and south west with a noticeable concentration of finds along the Iron Age shoreline.

As mentioned before, 84% of the finds occur within the modern boundaries of Lincolnshire. The figures by area are:

| | | % |
|---|---|---|
| North Lincolnshire | | |
| (north of Lincoln) | 327 | 61.5 |
| East Lincolnshire | | |
| (Partney/ Ulceby Cross area) | 82 | 15.4 |
| South Lincolnshire | | |
| (south of Lincoln) | 38 | 7.1 |
| | 447 | 84.0 |
| Norfolk | 33 | 6.2 |
| Cambridgeshire | 18 | 3.4 |
| Nottinghamshire | 8 | 1.5 |
| Northamptonshire | 7 | 1.3 |
| Yorkshire | 6 | 1.1 |
| Leicestershire | 4 | 0.8 |
| All other | 9 | 1.7 |
| | 532 | |

The figures demonstrate the concentration of finds in the north of Lincolnshire although this is somewhat distorted by major hoards. The 1994-1996 hoards at Caistor contained 85 units and all but one of the 60 finds from South Ferriby came from the 1904-1908 hoards.

Similarly all but two of the 40 Partney finds came from the 1988 hoard. By contrast, with the exception of the Hallaton hoard discussed below, there are no major hoards in the south of Lincolnshire and the 38 coins found here (as well as the 18 coins found in Cambridgeshire) come from scattered finds. Snettisham accounts for 22 of the 33 coins found in Norfolk.

Jeffrey May [13] noted that three sites in Lincolnshire contained pre-conquest pottery: Kirmington, Dragonby and Ancaster, and that a further three sites were major Iron age settlements: Ludford, South Ferriby and Ulceby Cross. Coin moulds for producing blanks have been discovered at Old Sleaford (one containing a pellet sufficient to mint a silver unit) and at Leicester.

A few generalisations may be made. The concentration of coins in the north of Lincolnshire argues for at least one northern mint. South Ferriby, known to be an important site and commanding the main crossing point of the Humber is an obvious candidate. Ludford which has produced a wide range of coins covering the entire series is another strong possibility as is Dragonby, a major Iron Age site, and Caistor. Clues to this latter site include the remarkable percentage of broken or fragmentary coins in the Caistor hoard (65%) possibly the discarded attempts of poor striking. Allied to this are the 4 clumsily engraved examples of type 33d, all from Caistor, which have every appearance of a trial production.

In the east of Lincolnshire the heavy concentration of units in the Partney/Ulceby Cross area indicates another probable mint site. In the south 4,290 fragments of pellet moulds have been discovered at Old Sleaford but only 13 units and 12 half units have been found there perhaps indicating that striking took place elsewhere.

Coin moulds have also been discovered at Leicester but only two units. However the discovery of 5,292 coins at Hallaton in Leicestershire 14 in 2000, including 147 boar/horse units, has brought this area into prominence. The deposit, or series of deposits, also included 4,583 inscribed Corieltavian coins and it is believed that the bulk of the deposits occurred in the first century AD.

A breakdown of the boar/horse coins in the find is interesting:

| | |
|---|---|
| Leins 1b. Early period Type 1a (VA 855-3, BMC 3194-3195) | 1 |
| Leins 3a. Late period horse right Types 24-26 | 57 |
| Leins 3b. Late period horse left Type 27 | 16 |
| Leins 5a. Late period horse right domino Type 31 | 1 |
| Leins 6b. Late period horse left kite Type 32 | 72 |
| | 147 |

Apart from the single early pierced boar type, all the coins are from the Late Period with an extraordinary number of left facing kite types (previously known from only 6 examples). If, as has been suggested, deposits at this site were "closely associated with ritual sacrifice and/or feasting"[15] perhaps the kite type held particular significance for the tribe living there.

It is now accepted that the term "Corieltavian" encompasses a number of separate tribal communities loosely falling within the general area of the "North East Coast". The later inscribed coins indicate the contemporary nature of many of the rulers. There appears to be no central mint which would imply a central authority. May[16] pointed out that there were 14 major nucleated settlements in the East Midlands, all evenly spaced with about 25 km between them. Any or all of these settlements may have minted coins and include South Ferriby, Dragonby, Kirmington, Owmby, Ludford and Partney/Ulceby Cross where major finds have been made. To these should be added the historically significant sites of Lincoln (*Lindum*) and Leicester (*Ratae Coritanorum*).

## Distribution of Half Units

Half units are even more concentrated in the north than units. Of the 246 examples known 216 were found in Lincolnshire: 175 (71%) north of Lincoln and only 19 (8%) in the east and 22 (9%) in the south.

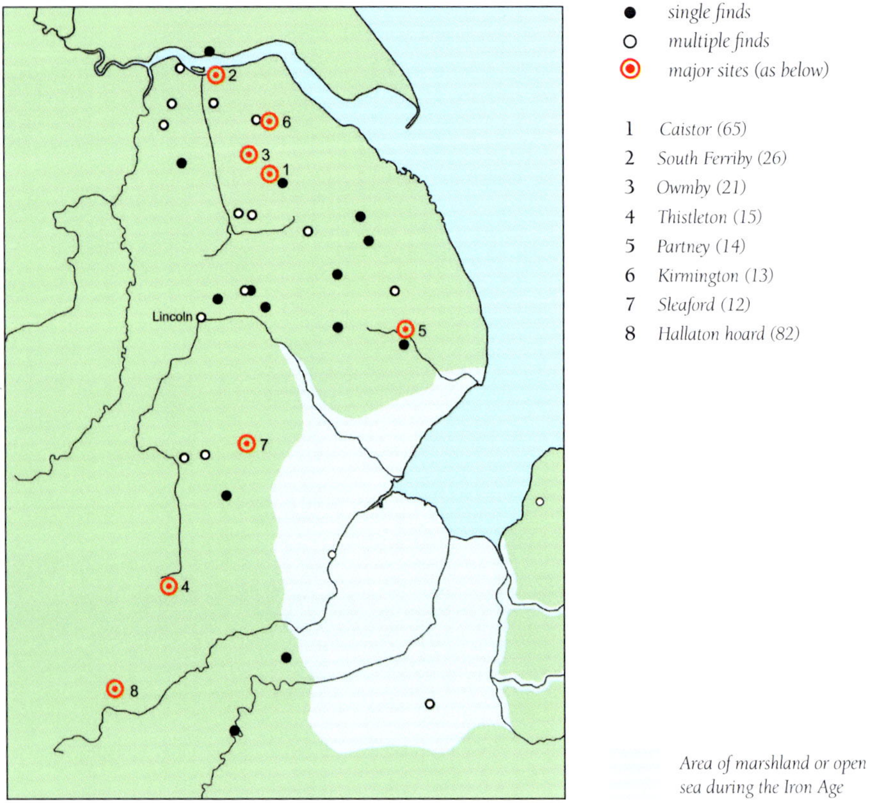


**20.** *Distribution of silver half units. Excludes finds outside the boundary of the map: Herefordshire (1), Hertfordshire (1), Kent (1), Norfolk (1), Suffolk (1)*

Caistor is again the major site with other major finds at South Ferriby, Kirmington, Owmby, and Partney mirroring the pattern of the units. Sleaford, a known settlement site, and the temple site of Thistleton feature prominently on the list; the relatively large number of half units found at the latter site (there are no units) may represent votive offerings.

The Hallaton hoard contained 82 boar/horse half units:

| | |
|---|---|
| Leins 2b. Late period Type horse left 33 | 1 |
| Leins 4a. Late period horse right Type 38 | 20 |
| Leins 4b. Late period horse left Type 37 | 48 |
| Leins 7a. Late period horse right kite Type 42 | 4 |
| Leins 7b. Late period horse left kite Type 41 | 9 |
| | 82 |

The four examples of Type 42 are the first examples known of a kite type with a left facing horse.

**22.** *Blank flan, 15-17mm, 1.02g, possibly for Corieltavian silver unit. Found Wragby, Lincs.*

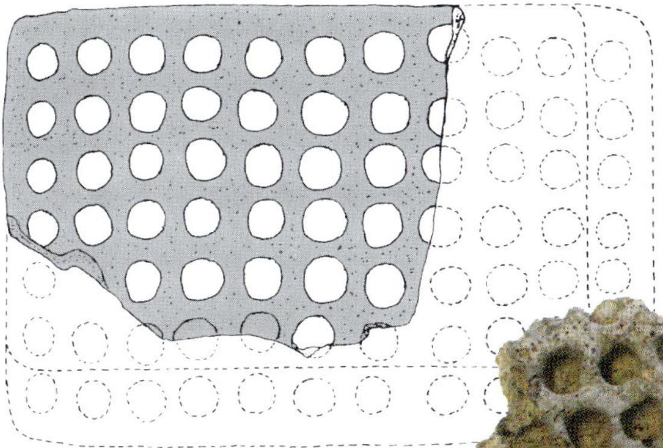

**21.** *Fragments of Corieltavian coin pellet moulds from Late Iron Age mint sites at Old Sleaford, Lincs., (above) and Blackfriars, Leicester.*

# Concordance - Units

| BM | VA | CCI | Type | Dies |
|---|---|---|---|---|
| 3194 | | 93.0789 | 1a | 6/5 |
| 3195 | | 68.0023 | 1a | 6/6 |
| - | 855-3 | 84.0759 | 1a | 6/5 |
| 3196 | | 68.0024 | 1b | 6/8 |
| - | 855-8 | 96.2101 | 3b | 12/21 |
| 3197 | | 93.0791 | 6a | 20/36 |
| 3198 | | 93.0802 | 17a | 58/98 |
| 3199 | | 93.0803 | 16b | x /89 |
| 3200 | | 93.0783 | 9b | 30/54 |
| 3201 | | 93.0790 | 2 | 8/15 |
| 3202 | 855-7 | 68.0022 | 4a | 13/24 |
| 3203 | | 93.0794 | 12a | 41/68 |
| - | 855-5 | 71.0007 | 9a | 29/53 |
| 3204 | | 93.0795 | 11b | 39/66 |
| 3205 | | 90.0823 | 8 | 28/51 |
| 3206 | | 93.0801 | 8 | 28/52 |
| 3207 | 857-3 | 63.0083 | 21a | 64/108 |
| - | 857-1 | 63.0084 | 21b | 66/111 |
| 3208 | 857-5 | 63.0085 | 16a | 51/83 |
| 3209 | | 93.0793 | 16a | 53/88 |
| 3210 | | 93.0805 | 16b | x /91 |
| 3211 | | 93.0804 | 16b | 52/90 |
| 3212 | 860-1 | 63.0093 | 15a | 48/77 |
| 3213 | 864-1 | 61.0073 | 7a | 25/42 |
| 3214 | | 68.0025 | 22a | 72/119 |
| - | 875-1 | 63.0095 | 22a | 72/119 |
| 3215 | 875-2 | 63.0094 | 22a | 70/118 |
| 3216 | | 63.0096 | 25a | 129/188 |
| 3217 | | 63.0122 | 26e | x /208 |
| 3218 | | 63.0099 | 24d | 105/152 |
| 3219 | 877-7 | 63.0098 | 24e | 110/157 |
| 3220 | | 63.0101 | 24e | x /177 |
| 3221 | | 63.0102 | 24e | 126/183 |
| 3222 | | 63.0103 | 24e | 125/182 |
| 3223 | | 63.0104 | 24e | x /163 |
| 3224 | | 63.0105 | 24e | x /166 |
| 3225 | | 63.0106 | 24e | 111/164 |
| 3226 | | - | 24e | 111/164 |
| 3227 | | 63.0100 | 24e | x /177 |
| - | 877-1 | 84.0758 | 24e | 114/170 |
| - | 877-5 | 61.0083 | 25c | x /191 |
| - | 887-1 | 61.0090 | 27b | x /214 |
| 3228 | 884-1 | 61.0093 | 28a | x /230 |
| 3229 | | 63.0126 | 28a | x /233 |
| 3230 | | 63.0123 | 26d | x /203 |
| 3231 | | 63.0124 | 26d | x /206 |
| 3232 | 877-3 | 61.0082 | 26d | x /204 |
| 3233 | | 90.0824 | 31 | x /245 |
| 3234 | | 93.0826 | 30 | x /242 |

| ABC | CCI | Type | Dies |
|---|---|---|---|
| 1779 | 04.2453 | 2 | 8/17 |
| 1782 | 08.8602 | 5c | 17/29 |
| 1785 | 04.2451 | 7a | 25/43 |
| 1788 | 96.3102 | 8 | 28/51 |
| 1791 | 96.3103 | 15b | 49/78 |
| 1794 | 95.3901 | 21d | 69/114 |
| 1797 | 74.0012 | 18a | 59/100 |
| 1800 | 96.1405 | 22a | 70/118 |
| 1803 | 00.1199 | 24e | 123/180 |
| 1806 | 99.0873 | 28a | x /221 |
| 1809 | 01.1595 | 27c | x /218 |
| 1812 | 00.0205 | 30 | x /242 |
| 1815 | 90.0824 | 31 | x /245 |
| 1818 | 01.1690 | 32a | x /246 |

x obliterated obverse die

**23.** *Rich Type 16a.*

**24.** *Rich Type 24.*

# Concordance - Half units

| BM | VA | CCI | Type | Dies |
|---|---|---|---|---|
| 3236 | | 92.0122 | 33a | 130/251 |
| 3237 | | 93.0799 | 33b | 130/252 |
| 3238 | | 73.0101 | 34a | 132/256 |
| 3239 | | 96.2175 | 34a | 132/255 |
| 3240 | | 63.0130 | 37b | x /273 |
| 3241 | | 63.0131 | 37a | x /265 |
| 3242 | | 96.2176 | 37a | x /265 |
| 3243 | | 73.0102 | 37a | x /269 |
| 3244 | | 68.0026 | 35a | 136/260 |
| 3245 | 862-1 | 93.0797 | 35a | 136/260 |
| 3246 | 889-1 | 74.0017 | 41a | x /338 |
| 3247 | 889-3 | 96.2174 | 41b | x /342 |
| - | 889-5 | 73.0099 | 41b | x /341 |
| 3248 | 889-7 | 73.0097 | 41c | x /345 |
| 3249 | | 93.0823 | 39b | x /325 |
| 3250 | | 74.0016 | 39b | x /325 |
| 3251 | | 73.0095 | 38f | x /299 |
| 3252 | | 93.0827 | 38f | x /298 |
| 3253 | | 96.2172 | 38f | x /301 |
| 3254 | | 96.2166 | 38g | x /318 |
| - | 879-1 | 61.0099 | 38g | x /317 |
| 3255 | | 96.2173 | 38f | x /299 |
| - | 866-1 | 69.0137 | (1) | |
| - | 867-1 | 85.0015 | (2) | |
| - | 881-1 | 63.0135 | (3) | |

| ABC | CCI | Type | Dies |
|---|---|---|---|
| 1821 | - | (4) | 25/42 |
| 1824 | 95.3450 | 33a | 130/249 |
| 1827 | 85.0096 | 35b | 137/261 |
| 1833 | 97.1326 | 38g | x /306 |
| 1836 | 00.0863 | 39b | x /326 |
| 1839 | 98.1924 | 41c | x /343 |
| 1842 | (5) | 42 | x /346 |

(1) Continental import
(2) Atrebatic, Danebury type
(3) too worn for classification
(4) Type 7a unit struck on an underweight flan
(5) Leins 2007 *BNJ*, page 45, 7a
x obliterated obverse die

**25.** *Rich Type 7a.*

**26.** *The Heckington Stag bronze figurine, 87mm, Romano-British, c.2nd-early 4th century AD, found near Kirkby le Thorpe, Lincs.*

**27.** *The Spilsby Stag. Or is it a horse with a shaggy barred mane? Rich Type 12a.*

## Endnotes

1. van Arsdell 1989 p. 236, Rudd & others 2010 p. 7 (phases 5-7).
2. Leins 2007 p. 38.
3. Crawford 1983 407/1, 407/2.
4. Compare CCI 03.0217 (dies 12/21) with 02.0614 (dies 13/21), 01.0845 (dies 12/22) with 98.1048 (dies 13/22) and 95.3011 (dies 12/23) with 94.0524 (dies 13/23).
5. DNW sale 5 October 2009 lot 5033, ABC 1782.
6. e.g. ABC 1501, 1516.
7. 371 examples out of the 734 (50.5%) that can be securely identified, compared to 162 (22.1%) in the Early Period, 48 (6.5%) in the Intermediate and 153 (20.8%) in the Late.
8. CCI 71.0008, 82.0152, 93.0805
9. CCI 74.0012 (1.43g), 93.0807 (1.38g), 04.0799 (1.32g).
10. Compare CCI 04.2643 (before the flaw) with 95.2682 (with the line between the forelegs) with 00.0194 (with the additional flaw at the tail).
11. Leins 2007 Appendix 1.
12. Leins 2007 Appendix 1.
13. May 1994 pp. 14-21.
14. Leins 2007.
15. Leins 2007 p.39.
16. May 1994 p. 18.

## Bibliography

Allen D.F. 1963 SCBI 3, *The Coins of the Coritani.*

Cottam E, de Jersey P, Rudd C, & Sills J., 2010, *Ancient British Coins.*

Crawford M.H. 1983, *Roman Republican Coinage.*

Cunliffe B.W. 2005 (4th edition), *Iron Age Communities in Britain.*

De Jersey P. 2001, *Celtic Coinage in Britain.*

Evans J. 1864, *The Coins of the Ancient Britons.*

Hobbs R. 1996, *British Iron Age coins in the British Museum.*

Leins I. 2007, Coins in Context: Coinage and Votive Deposition *in Iron Age South-east* Leicestershire, *BNJ* 77 pp. 22-48.

Mack R.P. 1975, *The Coinage of Ancient Britain.*

May J. 1989, Iron Age Coins in Yorkshire, from *Celtic Coinage: Britain and Beyond* Melinda Mays (ed.) pp. 93-111.

May J. 1994, Coinage and the Settlements of the Corieltauvi in East Midland Britain, *BNJ* 64 pp. 1-21.

Van Arsdell R.D, 1989 *Celtic Coinage of Britain.*

**28.** *This Norfolk Wolf Right gold stater (ABC 1393) of the Iceni – neighbours of the Corieltavi – probably inspired the Lincolnshire Wolf silver unit. Note the bird on the wolf's rump and smiling face below. Found Norfolk, 1997.* Chris Rudd List *30, January 1998, No.29.*

**29.** *Only coin in the series with no boar: the Lincolnshire Wolf, Rich Type 8. Extremely rare, distinctly Corieltavian. Struck to mark a treaty, royal marriage or victory over the Iceni? Found Wragby, Lincs.* Chris Rudd List *94, July 2007, No.33.*

# Appendix

### 1906 South Ferriby hoard

| Hoard No. | SCBI No. | CCI No. | BM No. | Type |
|---|---|---|---|---|
| 1 | 306 | 63.0096 | 3216 | 25a |
| 2 | 307 | 63.0097 | | 25b |
| 3 | 305 | 63.0125 | | 25c |
| 4 | 361 | 63.0132 | | 37a |
| 5 | 88 | 63.0130 | 3240 | 37b |
| 6 | 89 | 63.0131 | 3241 | 37a |
| 7 | 311 | 63.0109 | | 24e |
| 8 | 310 | 61.0072 | | 24d |
| 9 | 312 | 61.0074 | | 24e |
| 10 | 75 | 63.0101 | 3220 | 24e |
| 11/12 | 320/1 | * | | |
| 13 | 72 | 63.0098 | 3219 | 24e |
| 14 | 322 | * | | |
| 15 | 77 | 63.0103 | 3222 | 24e |
| 16/17 | 323/4 | * | | |
| 18 | 80 | 63.0106 | 3225 | 24e |
| 19 | 81 | ** | 3226 | 24e |
| 20 | 79 | 63.0105 | 3224 | 24e |
| 21 | 73 | 63.0099 | 3218 | 24d |
| 22 | 76 | 63.0102 | 3221 | 24e |
| 23 | 78 | 63.0104 | 3223 | 24e |
| 24 | 74 | 63.0100 | 3227 | 24e |
| 25/26 | 325/6 | * | | |
| 27 | 317 | 66.0036 | | 26a |
| 28 | | * | | |
| 29 | 85 | 63.0124 | 3231 | 26d |
| 30 | 319 | 63.0116 | | 26d |
| 31 | 318 | 63.0110 | | 26d |
| 32 | 83 | 63.0123 | 3230 | 26d |
| 33 | 82 | 63.0122 | 3217 | 26e |
| 34 | 329 | 68.0026 | 3244 | 35a |
| 35/36 | 330/1 | * | | |
| 37 | 86 | 63.0126 | 3229 | 28a |
| 38/39 | 342/3 | * | | |
| 40 | 347 | 61.0097 | | 28a |
| 41 | 341 | 63.0127 | | 28a |
| 42 | 353 | 63.0171 | | 38g |
| 43 | 374 | 63.0135 | | worn |
| 44 | 364 | 63.0133 | | 37a |
| 45 | 372 | 63.0134 | | 39a |

* not illustrated in SCBI

** not in the CCI

### coins from the 1905 hoard

| SCBI No. | CCI No. | Type |
|---|---|---|
| 308 | 61.0083 | 25c |
| 313 | 61.0075 | 24d |
| 332 | 61.0084 | 24e |
| 333 | 61.0077 | 24e |
| 334 | 61.0078 | 24e |
| 335 | 61.0085 | 24e |
| 336 | 61.0086 | 26d |
| 337 | 61.0087 | 26d |
| 338 | 61.0088 | 24e |
| 339 | 61.0089 | 24e |
| 340 | 61.0079 | 24e |
| 344 | 61.0094 | 28a |
| 345 | 61.0095 | 28a |
| 354 | 61.0080 | 38e |
| 355 | 61.0100 | 38e |
| 356 | 61.0101 | 38b |
| 362 | 61.0105 | 33a |
| 363 | 61.0106 | 37a |
| 365 | 61.0107 | 37a |
| 366 | 61.0108 | 37a |

### Summary

| | | |
|---|---|---|
| Units | 24d | 3 |
| | 24e | 18 |
| | 25a | 1 |
| | 25b | 1 |
| | 25c | 2 |
| | 26a | 1 |
| | 26d | 6 |
| | 26e | 1 |
| | 28a | 5 |
| Half Units | 33a | 1 |
| | 35a | 1 |
| | 37a | 6 |
| | 37b | 1 |
| | 38b | 1 |
| | 38e | 2 |
| | 38g | 1 |
| | 39a | 1 |
| Unidentified | | 12 |
| | | 64 |

# Type index

**30.** Turcos is *Celtic for 'boar', as in Gallic place-name* Turgon *(Charentes, W France), Gallic tribe* Cadurci, *originally* Catu-turci *'battle boars', and Celtiberian tribe* Roturkon *'big boars'. Above: silver drachm of the Cadurci, c.120-50 BC, with boar-tusked stylised head.*

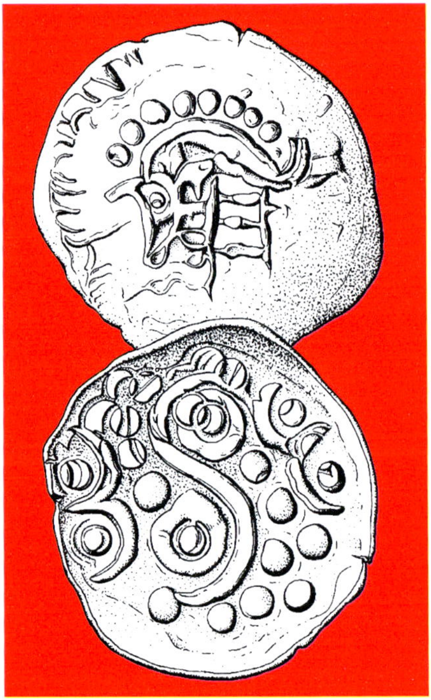

**31.** *The only Corieltavian gold coins to feature a boar, albeit stylised, are Lindsey Scyphate quarter staters (ABC 1767-73), first discovered in 1981 and thought to be bride price, nipple caps, blood cups or semen vessels. The S-shape also occurs on the earliest silver coins, Rich Type 1 and 2. Found Osbournby, Lincs., 1996.* Chris Rudd *List 29, 1997, No.47.*

ISBN 978-0-9566889-1-0

**A brief introduction to Ancient British coins. 56 pages, 300 coin photos, most greatly enlarged to aid identification. £10 from Chris Rudd.**

*This little book brings Celtic coins to life like no other and is a joy to read, packed with superb illustrations on every page.* DR JOHN SILLS

*A wonderfully illuminating introduction. Every page encourages the reader to ask questions and learn more.* PROFESSOR MARTIN HENIG

*The first concise guide to coins of the ancient Britons, clearly written with no waffle. A riot of colour.* DR PAUL SEALEY

*A perfect starting point. Profusely illustrated is an understatement.*
PROFESSOR VINCENT MEGAW

*It takes you through the minefield of Ancient British coins and leads you out the other side wanting more. A great little book.*
CHRISTOPHER WEBB

*Superbly produced, the perfect introduction.*
DAVID SEAR

*A must-have for all detectorists.* HARRY BAIN

*Large-format pictures make it possible to appreciate and identify these fascinating examples of our early monetary history.*
GUY DE LA BEDOYERE

*The perfect introduction. Beautifully illustrated throughout, packed full of incredible detail.*
DR MILES RUSSELL

*Highly attractive, beautifully illustrated, packed with interest and information on every page.*
DR JOHN DAVIES

*A must-have gallery and guide for anyone thinking about starting a collection of these miniature works of art.* BRETT HAMMOND

*A really useful wee book which offers a great and innovative introduction to the topic.*
DR FRASER HUNTER

*This authoritative handbook is a gem of synthesis. A snitch at £10.* ITALO VECCHI

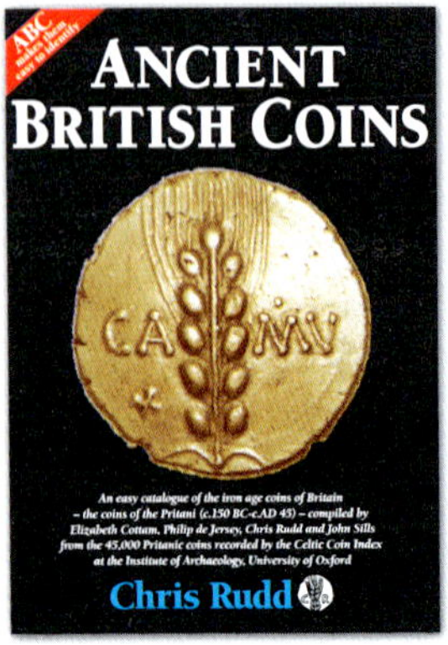


ISBN 978-0-09566889-0-3

**A comprehensive catalogue of Ancient British coins. Big hardback, 256 pages, 4000 coin photos including 2000 twice-size enlargements, plus 500 other illustrations, diagrams, tables and maps. £75 from Chris Rudd.**

*ABC is a remarkable achievement. It manages to combine scholarship and accessible information in a volume whose every page is interesting and whose writing style makes it fun to use.*

PROFESSOR MIRANDA ALDHOUSE-GREEN

*ABC provides a clear and stunningly illustrated catalogue that is a must for everyone interested in Britain's most intriguing artefacts. A great book.*

PROFESSOR SIR BARRY CUNLIFFE

*ABC is both a very useful and very beautiful book, full of crisp photographs of the best examples of British Iron Age coinage.*

PROFESSOR SHEPPARD FRERE

*Chris Rudd has reinvented the genre to make a very populist catalogue which is accessible to collectors and metal detectorists, while still containing all the arcane details, indexing and concordances to make ABC a valuable volume for scholars too.*

PROFESSOR JOHN CREIGHTON

*An indispensable aid to anyone wanting to identify British Iron Age coins and find out more about when and where they were made and used.*

PROFESSOR COLIN HASELGROVE

*There has never before been a British Celtic catalogue displaying a pictorial record of such uniformly high photographic and artistic quality as this.*

RAINER KRETZ

*ABC is very much more than just an outstandingly good catalogue. It is a lively and informative read in its own right and an extremely useful reference book.*
*I cannot recommend ABC too highly.*

DR DAPHNE NASH BRIGGS

*I can think of no other major piece of scholarship that is so accessible and user-friendly. You and your fellow authors wear your formidable knowledge with a modesty that does you great credit. ABC will endure for generations and is the sort of thing that justifies a lifetime.*

DR PAUL SEALEY